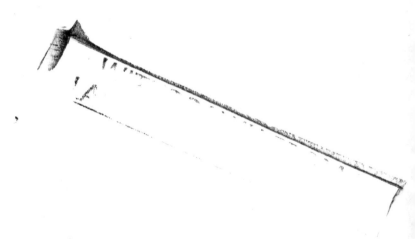

Discovering Inland Lancashire

Discovering
Inland Lancashire

RON & MARLENE FREETHY

JOHN DONALD PUBLISHERS LTD
EDINBURGH

ISBN 0 85976 000 0

British Library Cataloguing in Publication Data
Freethy, Ron
  Discovering Lancashire.
  1. Inland
  1. Lancashire (England). Travel
  I. Title II. Freethy, Marlene

04856330

PPR

Phototypeset by Newtext Composition Ltd, Glasgow.
Printed & bound in Great Britain by Scotprint Ltd, Musselburgh.

Introduction

Writing this book made us concentrate on Lancashire's past but also on its future, and the contrast could not be greater. In the 1960s and 1970s Lancashire had all the dirt and dereliction left by the Industrial Revolution; its coalmines were uneconomic and closing; its mill machinery was clapped out and uncompetitive; many of its rail links were run down and considered not worth the maintenance costs; its canals were silting up. Our relatives and friends searched for work, but had to stand in the dole queue and look at the rusting mine machinery, the dirty old mills, their windows broken and closed for ever. They sat on the canal banks and caught fish which they returned to the murky waters wondering how they ever managed to survive in such conditions.

During the 1970s only a few enlightened individuals were daft enough to feel that Lancashire could actually attract tourists. At worst they were treated with scorn both by the public in general and politicians in particular, and at best they were the victims of the dry 'Lankie humour'. Fancy organising canal cruises from Chorley or through the middle of Blackburn or Burnley or, even more incredibly, having an actual holiday on the Leeds to Liverpool canal. It's easy to understand the anger of millworkers who had been thrown out of their jobs and who then read of suggestions to turn their workplace into a museum! We realise that one generation must be replaced by the next before such schemes can be accepted. School visits to such places are invaluable in this respect.

The 1980s provided an essential breathing period during which the local people appreciated that the atmosphere was indeed cleaner, and there were good reasons to visit local mueums. Many of these such as Helmshore in Rossendale, Queen's Mill at Burnley and Trencherfield Mill at Wigan took the trouble to arrange working exhibits. This encouraged old operatives to show their grandchildren what life was like in the mills. At Helmshore, for example, there are many of the early textile machines including some from Arkwright's mill at Cromford. Also at Helmshore rallies of vintage cars and fire engines are held and draw large crowds. To get to these places visitors travel through the countryside and appreciate how beautiful the moorlands still are, and slowly but surely tourism becomes a viable proposition.

Thus the Lancashire of the 1990s is likely to go from strength to strength, and if this book helps in any way, we will feel well rewarded. We will also feel justified in having pestered the reference librarians of so many towns and asked so many questions of museum curators. All these people have been unstinting in their help, as have many of our friends. We thank Robert Smithies for the use of two of his photographs, Dudley Green for obtaining a copy of the Clitheroe Royal Grammar School charter, Bacup Natural History Society for the use of the photograph of the Ginny waggon and Bacup railway station. We thank their members for listening to our lectures on 'Old Lancashire and the Pennine Hills', and for providing tea for two eager researchers going through their archives.

We also thank the Editor of the *Lancashire Evening Telegraph* who has had the courage to publish our weekly column on 'The Lancashire Countryscene' for the last 20 years. Jim Ridge, the Curator of Ribchester's Roman Museum, has given us his friendship, his time, and the photograph of the Roman helmet.

Finally we thank the black labrador whose presence has ensured that each country walk mentioned in this book had to be properly explored and each nook and cranny properly 'sniffed out'.

Acknowledgement

The cover illustration of horse driving at Scorton is reproduced by permission of Bill Wilkinson, Press Photographer, Fulwood, Preston.

Contents

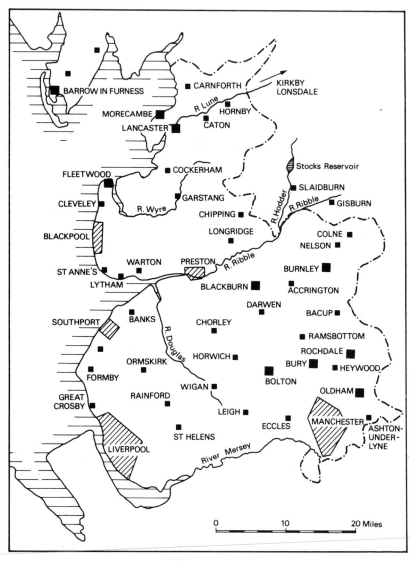

Location map.

CHAPTER 1

Lancashire's Heritage

Both of us are born and bred Lancastrians with one parent a true Mancunian, but with the boundary changes of 1974 one of us became a Cumbrian. Never mind, we love both counties and have strong allegiance to the Red Rose County, having lived within its confines for more than 30 years.

We travelled south for our education and knew that in these parts Lancashire meant smoke and mills, with hundreds of small quarries which provided gritstone for mills, paving stones and setts for town streets. It also meant disused canals, cotton and coal. We quickly learned that our accent was 'thowt queer' but no worse than that of Yorkshire-folk. Then the Roses rivalry was forgotten and the two Northern counties joined hands to repel boarders.

Lancashire and Yorkshire are divided by the sweeping Pennine Hills which earn their name of the 'Backbone of Old England', Yorkshire faces the full force of the drying wind blasting over the North Sea, whilst Lancashire soaks up the mositure-laden clouds wafted over the Atlantic and the Irish Sea. This accounts for Lancashire's fortune being made from cotton rather than remaining a weaver of wool like Yorkshire. Cotton fibres are much easier to handle in a damp atmosphere.

As most of the Red rose towns had similar origins, it makes sense to tell the story of industrial development and the growth of the cotton industry in general before going on in later chapters to describe individual towns and the often surprising amount of delightful countryside which surrounds them.

Compared to many counties, including Yorkshire, the name Lancashire came into being relatively late. It was formed in 1168 by the absorption of large areas of what was then Cheshireshire and the now long-extinct Eurwickshire, whilst later the Furness district was added as part of the Barony of Kendal. It was this latter area which was absorbed by the new county of Cumbria in the boundary changes of 1974, Lancashire was, however, compensated for its loss by the swallowing up of bits of reluctant Yorkshire including Gisburn, Barnoldswick and Saddleworth. The dust raised by both these decisions has still not completely settled, and they probably will not be accepted for another two generations.

Until the Industrial Revolution, Lancashire was sparsely populated, earning its living from sheep farming and the weaving of wool, the two usually being carried on together in remote hillside farmsteads and cottages. The commercial origins of both occupations take us back to the days of the abbeys prior to their dissolution in the mid-sixteenth century. Weavers' cottages are still a feature of hamlets and villages on the slopes of both the Yorkshire and Lancashire Pennines. Although Celts, Romans, Angles, Saxons, Scandinavians and Normans all settled here, they made little impact on the land we now call Lancashire. It was only when the large mills powered first by water and then by steam became efficient, that workers were attracted down from their weaving cottages on the hillside and then the environment changed. Apart from its climate, Lancashire also proved to have coal to fire the huge boilers powering the mills. In the late nineteenth century Lancashire had more than 400 mines which together yielded 13 million tons of coal each year, with reserves estimated to last for 250 years. Soon the factories grew larger, and back-to-back houses were built by the owners around their mills; the coal was carried from the mines on the hillsides first by Ginny waggons running down inclines direct to the mills, then as local supplies diminished, by canal and later by rail.

Smoke and soot polluted the air, and what were once glorious river valleys became areas of dirt and squalor, but where there was muck, there was certainly plenty of brass. The early attempts to dissipate the smoke entailed building ever taller and taller chimneys which were first evocatively described as 'smoke pokes'. But all this did was to spread the grime farther and farther into the countryside. It is not surprising to find that acid rain was first described by chemists at Manchester University in the 1850s. So much for those who thought it was a problem first noticed in the 1980s and destined to be a talking point of the '90s. The Lancashire towns were obviously worried as early as the 1850s when their new buildings and statues as well as the ancient churches began to

Haulage chains transported Ginny wagons of coal from the mines down into the mill towns. This photograph shows Old Meadows Colliery near Bacup.

crumble from the effects of the smoke and fumes.

The voice of industry, the full employment and the increasing demand for Lancashire textiles stifled any semblance of criticism, and as the Victorian age of prosperity peaked, only a few cranks ever mentioned environmental damage, and a Safety at Work Act was more than a century away from even being thought about. There were periods of decline, notably during the American Civil Wars of the 1860s when the loss of the American crop led to the Lancashire

Cotton Famine. For the most part, though, cotton indeed was king!

What is cotton and why did Lancashire dominate the world scene for so long? Cotton belongs to a family of plants known as the Malvacea which also includes the mallows. Two species, or rather hybrids between the two, are the basis of the modern crop – these are *Gossypium hirsutum* and *Gossypium barbadense,* Geneticists, with huge profits available to the successful, have produced plants which grow quickly and are resistant to pests and disease, whilst establishing which strains would grow best in which areas of the world had also to be established. Another property which also had to be taken into account was how well the fibres would spin, and the 'brittleness factor' took some time to breed out of the commercial strains.

All strains of cotton require at least six months free from frost with plenty of sunshine, but also there need to be periods of substantial watering either by rainfall or by irrigation. Cotton is therefore best grown between latitudes of 45°N and 30°S, which takes in Kazakhastan in Russia in the north to Australia and Argentina in the south. The seed is planted in the spring and is ready for harvesting between six and seven months later. Flowering occurs within about six weeks and the seed pods develop from the withered flowers and are known as 'bolls' consisting of up to 30 seeds, each protected by a mat consisting of 20,000 to 30,000 cotton fibres. About two months after setting the bolls burst and the fibres can be separated. The fibre separated from the seed is called 'lint' and this is sold according to the average length of the fibres which is known as its 'staple'. It is these staples which determine how fine the yarn spun from them will be. 'Asiatic' strains are short, being below 26mm, whilst the American 'upland' strains are of medium length, between 26mm and 29mm. The long 'Egyptian' strains are between 30mm and 38mm, whilst the West Indian 'Sea Island' strains are extra long and always exceed 39mm.

Some 34 million hectares, which is 2.3% of the world's cultivated lands, are devoted to cotton, and despite increased demand the area under cotton has not increased due to the geneticist's work guaranteeing greater yields. The yield has risen from around 250 kilos of lint per hectare to over 500 kilos per hectare in most areas, whilst Israel has achieved the

Pictures taken in the early years of the twentieth century show:
Above: A typical spinning mill near Todmorden.
Below: Typical weaving sheds in the Rossendale Valley.

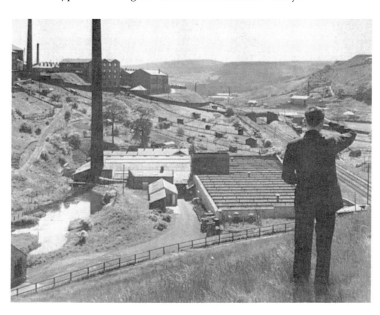

astounding yield of around 1500 kilos per hectare, China is the world's largest producer. Although most of the crop, especially in undeveloped countries, is still harvested by hand, expensive and sophisticated machines are used in some areas.

The newly picked crop is known as seed cotton, and separating the fibres from the seed was a backbreaking job, but in 1794 Eli Whitney, an American plantation owner, developed a machine which he called a 'gin' to do this job. A more highly developed form of this engine is still in use to the present day. The lint is then compressed into huge bales, each weighing around 220 kilos and it is these which once poured into Liverpool and along the canals to the Lancashire mills. At one time the seeds were thrown away but these days they are crushed to produce high-quality vegetable oil which is used for cooking and as a base for the cosmetics industry. Even the residue from this crushing is used, and is being milled to produce animal fodder; and in some countries it is even added to flour for low-quality but cheap bread.

Textiles have been found in Mexico dating to 5800 BC and in Pakistan to 3000 BC. Archaeologists have worked out that they were made from wild undeveloped cotton plants. By 500 BC India was exporting high-quality cotton, and Herodotus, writing in 445 BC, called cotton 'tree wool' and indicated its importance in the Greek world of commerce. We still refer to 'cotton wool', and in Germany cotton is known as Baumwoolle. The use of cotton spread through Europe following the Crusades, and it was from the Arabic word 'Qutun' that the English word 'cotton' and the Fench 'katoen' derived.

Whilst the finest cloth was then still exported from India, the Flemish weavers of cotton were also famous, but a series of religious persecutions in this part of Europe caused many to move to England and a settlement was centred in and around Manchester. It was very much a cottage-based industry, however, sometimes running parallel with the production of woollen garments, although the provision of raw material for the latter was much more reliable, with cotton imports still entirely a matter of chance. It was in eighteenth-century Britain that mechanisation evolved surprisingly quickly, and Lancashire held an unparalleled dominance in textiles until the 1950s when an irreversible decline set in. It was the Lancashire

This old photograph of Burnley shows how self-sufficient a cotton town could be. Note the canal and the railway with the coal mine on the left providing fuel for the mills which polluted the atmosphere.

lads whose inventions fuelled the Industrial Revolution.

In 1733 John Kay invented the flying shuttle which doubled the output of a handloom and enabled cottage operatives to earn a better living. Far less welcome was the Spinning Jenny, invented by James Hargreaves in 1767, the water frame of Richard Arkwright in 1769, and the spinning mule of Samuel Crompton in 1779 which enabled one machine to produce dozens of threads or yarns. Inevitably this led to over-production as the home market became saturated – the export trade via Liverpool had not yet developed. The handloom weavers first became worried and then violent, leading to the Luddite riots during which new machines were smashed. Things were made worse in 1784 as Edmund Cartwright developed a power loom which by 1830 had rendered the handloom extinct. Running parallel with these innovations was the demand for bleached cloth which had previously been produced only by long exposure to sunlight. New bleaching processes were invented and also new methods of chemically dying textiles, and the spent chemicals were simply drained into the same rivers which provided either the direct water or the steam derived from it to drive the machines. As people left the hillside villages to work in the mills along the valley floor, their sewage also emptied into the rivers.

Here, then, is a portrait of Victorian Lancashire. Smoke, noise, long hours of grinding toil, polluted rivers, busy but grimy canals, and railways. The scene was faithfully recorded by Frederick Engels, Karl Marx, Mrs Gaskell and Charles Dickens, who all wrote critically about Manchester.

The commercial production of cotton involved two processes – spinning and weaving. Some towns such as Oldham specialised in spinning and the multi-storey mills are typical. Other towns such as Burnley became weaving specialists, and here there were many single-storeyed weaving sheds with skylights ensuring good vision for the operatives. The long side of Burnley's Turf Moor football ground is still called 'The Shed'.

The history of the industry is recorded in many museums in the county. At Queen's Mill in Burnley a steam-powered cotton mill is still working, and reminders of the handloom weaving industry also remain in upland villages. At Helmshore near Haslingden there is a museum describing both the woollen and the cotton industries. At Trencherfield Mill at Wigan a huge steam engine is still fired regularly and attracts visitors from the Wigan Pier Museum.

The village of Wycoller, once an important centre of the wool trade from which packhorse trails can still be followed to the Yorkshire markets at Heptonstall and Halifax, encapsulates the Lancashire story, past and present.

Still described as Lancashire's lost village, Wycoller is on the outskirts of Colne. From the town follow the A6068 road towards Keighley. There are two routes leading to the Country Park. A right turn leads through Trawden and the brown signs are followed to an extensive car park above the village. The alternative route is to continue to Laneshaw Bridge. Turn right (again indicated by a brown sign) and drop down to the bridge. Once again there is a choice. A right turn along Carriers Row joins the Trawden road and the car park. Following the road towards Haworth leads to another brown sign indicating the second Wycoller Car Park.

We remember the 1960s when Wycoller was truly a deserted village. A copy of the *Rambler magazine* of April 1906 takes us

This picture of Colne, taken in 1990, shows how mill towns have become cleaner with the decline of the cotton industry plus the effects of the clean air acts.

back even further and describes it under 'Disappearing Landmarks' but using the spelling Wycollar: 'Wycollar is the name given to a pretty dene or valley lying near Nelson, not far from the county of broad acres viz., Yorkshire, Down this lovely valley flows a stream that –

> Chatters over stony ways in little sharps and trebles,
> That bubbles into eddying bays and babbles on the pebbles.'

Whilst the *Rambler* account shows a few signs of poetic licence, there is no doubt that the village is one of the most historic in Britain, and we must be grateful that the setting-up of the Country Park has saved it. Many houses, once derelict, have been tastefully restored and Wycoller now feels happy and lived in.

The best approach is from the car park on the Colne side and following a neat path lined by trees leading down into Wycoller. Parking is restricted in the village itself, although there is, sensibly, space left for those holding a disabled badge. Look out on the right-hand side for a 'hedge' made out of huge slabs of stone. This relates to when Wycoller was a vaccary or cattle farm. Indeed the name derives from the word 'wyc' meaning a dairy farm and 'alr' meaning alder. Thus we have a dairy farm among the alders with stone field boundaries which have been dated to between 1100 and 1400 AD, although some historians have suggested that they may even be Saxon in origin.

The record of even earlier civilisations in the valley has been established by the work of the local archaeologists. Small flints have been found on the moors above the village which prove that folk were settled here in the Mesolithic period around 9000 years ago. Other artefacts including hammer stones and querns have been found and dated to around 3000 BC. These tools enabled the people to fell trees, an accelerating trend which has continued ever since.

In the village there are now coffee and craft shops, the ruins of Wycoller Hall, three historic bridges, and a well-appointed Information Centre depicting the history of the area and having an exhibition of old farm implements and a display of local natural history. It is strange that in the *Rambler* account of 1906 the ruins of Wycoller Hall are described, but it fails to mention that it was well known to Charlotte Brontë who used it as the inspiration for her Ferndean manor in *Jane Eyre*.

Each of the three bridges is a gem in its own right. The packhorse bridge dates from when Wycoller was a village earning its living from handloom weaving. The clapper bridge was also a vital crossing for the villagers, but the oldest of the bridges, the so-called Clam bridge, is beyond Wycoller on the track to Haworth. It has been suggested that this structure dates to the Iron Age; it is a huge slab of stone spanning the stream. The river is also crossed by a shallow ford, the only access to the upland farms.

If the historian is guaranteed fun, this area should not be ignored by the naturalist. In summer the hedgerows are coloured by a great variety of flowers, and breeding birds include dipper, kingfisher, both pied and grey wagtail, and the occasional common sandpiper. A delightful resident mammal is the water vole, a vegetarian described in *The Wind in the Willows* as Ratty. The fact that Ratty lives on Wycoller Beck means that the water is clean and unpolluted. As we have seen, pollution was a product of mass production, small-scale enterprises

Wycoller – a typical handloom weaving village with the packhorse bridge in the background. The ruins of Wycoller Hall can just be seen to the right.

having usually been in balance with the environment.

Wycoller, then, is a place to find wild nature as well as literary and historical associations, but what about ghosts and things that go 'bump' in the night? There is supposed to be a ghost horseman dressed in the clothes of the Stuart period who gallops through the village, over the packhorse bridge and up to the Hall. Legend has it that this is a one-time squire of the Hall returning to the scene of a dastardly crime. He is said to have murdered his wife on a dark wet night. The squire's ghost enters the hall and this is followed by the groans of his victim. The unfortunate lady herself is said to appear in ghostly form also and is known as 'Black Bess'.

Visitors to present-day Wycoller will probably not see the Stuart Squire or Black Bess, but there is much else to see and prove beyond doubt that the once lost village has been given the kiss of life and not the kiss of death!

And so back to the county as a whole. Just as the days of the handloom weaver came to an end, so eventually came the demise of the mills, with markets being lost to Third World countries with cheaper labour. Outdated machinery was not replaced as orders fell, and by the 1980s only a fraction of the

Many cottages in Wycoller would have had looms such as this in the days before the industrial revolution attracted country folk to the towns.

specialist mills remained. This meant less smoke belching into the atmosphere, while the Clean Air Acts of the 1950s began to have their effect. Bleach mills and dye works also closed down, whilst modern sewage disposal plants reduced the outflow into rivers, so that Lancashire's watercourses became cleaner. The canals which had fallen into dereliction are at long last being restored for pleasure craft, and many mill buildings have been given other tasks to perform. At last in the 1990s Lancashire is responding to the demands of tourism and now realises what it has to offer the naturalist and the historian. It might just be that where there is a *lack* of muck, there may *also* be brass!

CHAPTER 2

Manchester and Salford

To the average Lancastrian, if there is such a beast, Manchester means struggling through traffic jams and joining the crowds filling the shops or milling around the Old Trafford football or cricket grounds. Whatever the memory, it always involves the hustle and bustle of a city. There is, however, peace still to be found around the cathedral which was once a village church surrounded by moors and green fields, or in the comfort of a boat cruising along the Irwell or one of the canals which flow under the bridges. From these vantage points some idea of Old Manchester, the wool weaving village, can still be appreciated.

Ancient settlements were built to satisfy two main criteria: firstly, they had to be easily defended, and secondly the road and water communication systems must be good. The village of Manchester was set at the confluence of three rivers. The Irk and the Medlock first met and then fed the Irwell. The Irwell was perfectly navigable for ships of the size in use up to fairly modern times, and by then the Manchester Ship Canal was maintaining the essential link with the sea. The settlement was separated by the Pennine Hills from Yorkshire, and to the west the approach was made difficult by the then vast expanse of Chat Moss at the end of which was the River Mersey, the name of which simply means boundary river. Chat Moss was remote enough to have been as frightening as anything dreamed up by Sir Arthur Conan Doyle, who was educated at Stonyhurst College (see Chapter 10). It was not tamed until George Stephenson laid a railway across it by supporting the line on a raft of willow twigs. Peat cutting was a local industry, and at Risley Moss near Warrington, which is open free of charge on most days of the year, there are exhibitions devoted to local natural history and the peat-digging industry. There is an extensive and well laid-out Nature Reserve with good facilities for the disabled. The habitat is wet enough to be ideal for many water-based birds including resident moorhens and summer visiting warblers plus a delightful selection of butterflies and dragonflies. The Mosslands in pre-railway days ensured that Manchester stood at the only gateway to the west coast of Northern England.

The Brigantes, a tribe of Ancient Britons, held the banks of the Irwell before they were either forcibly overcome or perhaps peacefully annexed around 55 BC following the Roman invasion. It was the Romans who built Mamucium during the reign of Julius Agricola (AD 78 to 86), which means the 'place of the breast-like hill' and relates to the sandstone outcrop on which it stands. Soon afterwards the name seems to have been changed to Mancunium. The Roman fort was sited in the Castlefield area close to what is now Bridgewater Street and the terminus of the Rochdale Canal. Recent excavations have rescued a fraction of what must have been a substantial settlement swamped beneath centuries of subsequent buildings, no doubt making use of Roman stonework. Reminders of its importance can be seen from the network of roads which radiate from it. The route from modern Knutsford into Castlefield was part of the road known to the Romans as Watling Street,and this continued north through what is now Strangeways and Prestwich. The present section of the A6 to Stockport and on to Buxton and the south was also Roman in origin, as was the route across the Irwell to Salford and also the route into Yorkshire which now passes through Failsworth, Rochdale and over Blackstone Edge to the modern town of Huddersfield. The Blackstone Edge section of this road is also discussed in Chapter 3. From this it can be seen that Manchester was a vital crossroads between such settlements as Chester, Ribchester, Ilkley and Lancaster.

Manchester did not fade into obscurity following the departure of the Romans and had a chequered and none too peaceful history prior to the arrival of the Normans. During this time the name went through several variations including Mamucium, Maniyecastre and Mamecestre. The still quite small settlement suffered badly at the hands of the Danes in AD 870, and about 40 years after this devastation the son of Alfred the Great, Edward the Elder, sent a force of Mercians from the town of Thelwall in Cheshire to restore it and to occupy what was left of the Roman fort. Motorway travellers passing over the Thelwall viaduct do not usually realise that below them was

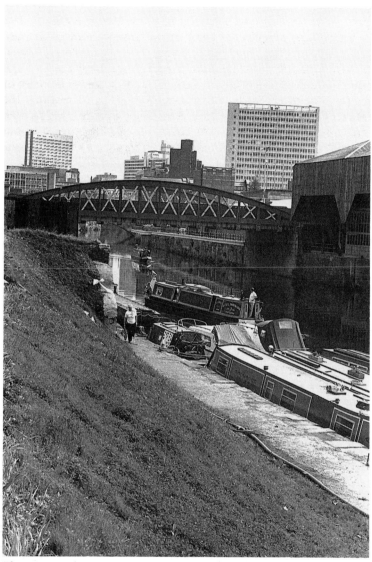

Pleasure cruisers on the River Irwell almost in the centre of Manchester behind the Granada TV studios.

one of the most important places in Saxon history.

Lancashire was divided later into six hundreds, each with, as the name implies, one hundred subservient manors. Salford was a hundred and Manchester on the opposite bank of the Irwell was subservient to it, which certainly accounts for a lot of local bitterness with Salford now merely a suburb of Manchester. In view of this it does seem strange that Salford did not have a church until 1635, its spiritual needs being served from the parish church of St. Mary's Manchester overlooking the Irwell on its raised site, and now elevated to cathedral status. The area is still known as St Mary's Gate even after all these years, but at the time of its Norman foundation it would just have been a small village church surrounded by farms and the focus of an important market and hosting the occasional fair day and a rushbearing. The latter ceremony dates to the days when churches had no form of heating and no stone floors, so the often muddy and wet nave was strewn with rushes gathered from the hills and these were ceremonially replaced each year. Nor did churches have seats, the strong standing in the centre of the nave whilst 'the weakest went to the wall', and leaned against it.

Like most of the sparsely populated North of England, the Salford hundred was given by William of Normandy to Roger de Poitou, The Knight did not fare so well at the hands of Henry I and 1102 he was banished. As Roger's lands were divided, Salford was retained by the Crown and the Queen is still Lady of the Royal Manor of Salford, whilst Manchester was given to the more loyal Grelley family with Robert the fifth Baron being the first to live there and building a manor house on the site now occupied by Chetham's School. On the nearby River Irk a corn mill was constructed and Manchester began to grow both in population and prosperity. From the manor house ran a ditch known as a dene, from which the modern thoroughfare known as Denesgate or Deansgate evolved.

Robert Grelley led a very active life and was present during the signing of Magna Carta by King John in 1215. John was never one to keep his word and stripped Robert of his lands, but fortunately the King died before this decree could be put into effect. Robert lived on in great splendour and in 1227 his Manchester was important enough to be granted a fair by

The Wellington Inn – One of Manchester's old buildings still standing. Photographed in 1949.

Henry III. Its market charter came in 1301 when Thomas Grelley was Lord of the Manor, by which time Manchester had spawned a number of smaller manors including Ashton-under-Lyne, Heaton Norris, Withington, Blackley, Gorton, Crumpsall, Ardwick, Openshaw, Clayton and Didsbury. Now that they have been swallowed up by the sprawl of the city, it is hard to imagine the local people travelling through green fields and woodlands and arriving along Toll Lane (now called St. Ann Street) to pay their taxes. The annual fair was held on the appropriately named Acresfield, which is now St. Ann's Square!

Although now one of the most popular shopping areas in the city, Acresfield (or perhaps Ann's Field) was still arable until the early eighteenth century when Lady Ann Bland erected a church which was consecrated by the Bishop of Chester in 1712. This meant that the area had to be enclosed, but a wide area had to be retained in order for the annual fair to be held. Bonnie Prince Charlie rode into the square in 1745, at which time it was still a rural spot, but by the 1870s all the trees had gone, and shops and public buildings had replaced private residences. From 1810 St. Ann's was the starting point for

Hackney carriages which could operate under licence over a radius of four miles.

This brief look at St. Ann's takes us on too quickly through the history of the city which became prosperous because of textiles. When did this industry come to the little village on the banks of the salmon-rich Irwell? The answer is 'gradually', but its development was due to the kindly guidance of its Lords of the Manor. When Thomas Grelley died in 1313 the manor was inherited by his sister Joan who was married to Sir John La Warr, whose brother Thomas was a priest and was rector of the church. He proved an excellent choice as previous rectors had been absentee priests eager to accept the tithes but not to work for the church. The La Warrs did well for Manchester, encouraging both trade and education, and in 1421 a Royal licence was granted to endow Manchester as a College of Clergy. A warden and eight fellows looked after the spiritual and educational needs of the people, and a feature of the Cathedral to this day is its width, a sign of the additions made to the medieval church to provide space for the work of the College.

After the failure of the male line in 1427, the La Warrs' lands including Manchester passed via the distaff (female) side to the West family who were far too occupied with the events of the Wars of the Roses to be anything other than absentee landlords. The family, however, is important in the annals of Manchester. The 15th Baron, Thomas West, was a friend of Henry VII who was once entertained at Manchester whilst on his way to see his mother the Countess of Richmond who was the second wife of the Earl of Derby, a member of the influential Stanley family who played such a vital role in Lancashire's history. Derby had a son by his first marriage who became Warden of Manchester College from 1481 to 1509, when he became Bishop of Ely. It is said that he obtained the latter post solely by influence and that he was illiterate, but whilst this may be true, he did nothing but good for the church in Manchester. He brought wood carvers from France including the remarkable Richard Bexwicke, and they produced some of the most amusing yet exquisite choir stalls to be found anywhere in the country. Despite this and the building of chantry chapels and a chapter house, he was not

Queen Victoria arriving on board the Admiralty yacht *Enchantress* to open the Manchester Ship Canal on 21st May 1894.

buried in the main church, but outside in the Stanley chapel as befitted someone who had been excommunicated before his death in 1525. It seems that he offended the church by 'living all the winter at Somersham with one who was not his sister and who wanted nothing to make her his wife save marriage'.

It seems that this turbulent priest may have been a lecherous illiterate, but he certainly appreciated art and obviously had a sense of humour. Only he could have approved the designs on the choir stalls which include rabbits roasting the huntsman, monkeys stealing from a pedlar's pack, people playing backgammon and, perhaps most significant of all, a wife chasing her husband who has obviously spilled his ale.

Perhaps industry came too quickly for Lancashire, and for Manchester in particular, with the result that no thought of planning entered the minds of industrialists and soon the pretty village became a town of utter squalor. It is no wonder that Manchester spawned disease, poverty and industrial unrest. Not all observers were happy, especially Sir James Kay, a doctor who later became Sir James Kay-Shuttleworth following his marriage into the ranks of the Shuttleworth family of Gawthorpe Hall in Padiham. He was active in promoting the Education Act of 1872 and was involved in the setting up of St Mark's, the first teachers' training college in London in the 1840s which one of us attended in the 1960s.

He knew from first hand the strikes, the poverty and the grinding 12-hour days which many children worked in the mills when they should have been enjoying a basic education.

In 1819 there was a meeting in the town which has been called Peterloo, bringing back grizzly memories of Waterloo which had been fought only four years before. Peterloo, however, was not a battle between two trained armies, but the butchery of working men meeting to demand some rights. They failed, eleven people were killed and hundreds were injured as sabre-wielding troops ploughed into the heart of the crowd.

This bloody, and probably unnecessary, event, caused by the commander-in-chief over-reacting, almost certainly spawned the *Manchester Guardian* in 1821 which soon built up a reputation for fighting hard for constitutional reform. John Bright and Richard Cobden helped to set up the Anti-Corn Law League in 1838 and the Free Trade Hall standing on the site of the Peterloo massacre was built two years later as its headquarters. The conditions led to writers such as Dickens and Mrs Gaskell, whose husband was a Unitarian minister in Manchester, to describe the squalor, and it was here that Engels

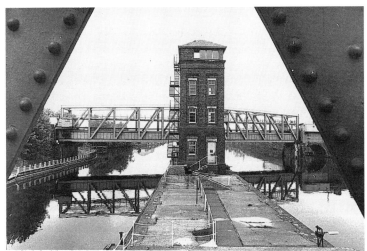

The Barton Swing Aqueduct – a remarkable feat of engineering.

and Karl Marx formulated their ideas on communism.

The first Free Trade Hall was a wooden structure which was replaced in 1843 by brick, but following the repeal of the Corn Laws at a time when Robert Peel was Prime Minister in 1849, it became the headquarters of the Atheneum Society. The first meeting was chaired by Charles Dickens, and later chairmen were Disraeli and Emerson. A third building, constructed in 1856, was almost totally destroyed by German bombs in 1940 but was reconstructed behind the magnificent facades. Open to the public at all times, part of the hall is the home of the world-renowned Hallé Orchestra, which is one of the many reminders that Manchester bred music as well as muck, art as well as agitated artisans, and science as well as smog.

There are six galleries sited in the city itself and in what were once outlying villages now swallowed by the city. The City Art Gallery was designed by Sir Charles Barry, an entirely fitting building to house a fine collection of European paintings. English artists represented include Hogarth, Gainsborough, Reynolds, Constable, Holman Hunt, Millais and L S Lowry, a local lad who painted industrial Lancashire as nobody else could.

The Queen's Park Art Gallery has some bronzes by Rodin

and an Epstein figure, 'Youth Advances', which was commissioned for the Festival of Britain in 1951. There is also one of the country's finest exhibitions of Victorian paintings and sculptures.

But our favourite four galleries are outside the city centre, and we love them because the buildings in which they are housed are reminders of life in the old villages. Wythenshawe Hall is splendidly half-timbered and was mainly constructed in the sixteenth century but it has also had a number of facelifts and restorations in the centuries which followed. It is entirely fitting that it should display Elizabethan furniture and ceramics including Staffordshire and English Delph. There are also displays of local history and some rather fine English and European paintings.

Heaton Hall at Prestwich was built in 1772 for the Earl of Wilton by the architect James Wyatt. An organ built by Samuel Green in 1792 is still in use and graces one of the finest Georgian houses in the country surrounded by a delightful park. Families wandering around the Hall soak up the glories of furniture, ceramics, watercolours, silver and glassware. It is more a process of osmosis than education.

The Fletcher Moss Museum doubles as a heritage centre and art gallery and is housed in the Old Parsonage at Didsbury. Here are displayed the very best of Manchester's collection of watercolours including works by David Cox, Paul Sandby and, above all, Turner, who travelled so much and worked so hard in the north-western districts of early nineteenth-century England. Those who are interested in costume should not miss visiting Platt Hall at Rusholme, a Georgian mansion built for the Worsley family. Here the Gallery of English Costume has an immense collection from the early seventeenth century right up to the present day.

The Whitworth Art Gallery in Oxford Road back in the city is administered by the University and has an excitingly large collection of prints and engravings dating back to the fifteenth century, plus textiles and embroideries. There are also some good English watercolours.

The University also has played its part in the scientific world; it was here in 1806 that the Quaker, John Dalton, worked out the Atomic Theory, and Rutherford first worked here to split

Whilst constructing the Barton Swing Aqueduct in 1890 this fine example of a dug-out canoe was unearthed.

the atom. It is no wonder that Manchester has some of the finest science museums outside London, all open to the public. The reputation also of the G Mex Centre, once the Central Station, is increasing quickly, and it has an exhibition area as good as any in the country.

Manchester has more than its share of libraries, all of which have been haunted by the pair of us squirreling away in search of Old Lancashire. We don't care much for Greater Manchester or Merseyside as county names. Give us Old Lancashire any time with its two glorious cities of Manchester and Liverpool, the latter described in a companion volume.

The Chetham Library is a friendly spot, but open only by appointment. It was founded near the church in the village in 1653 and was actually the first free public library in Europe. Humphrey Chetham was a prosperous merchant but a true philanthropist who at one time owned Turton Tower near Bolton (see Chapter 6). 'Books for all' was his philosophy at a time when the printing industry was very much in its infancy. The early presses had their letters fashioned out of wood and were kept in cases close to the press. Capital letters were kept in the upper case and small letters kept in the lower case – these early terms are still in use today even though typesetting is now done electronically. Chetham provided libraries in Manchester and Bolton, and the building which carries his name now houses over 100,000 books and manuscripts.

The John Rylands Library, which is open to the public, is also of world renown and resulted from the resources accumulated by a weaver from Wigan. It was his wife who founded the library to commemorate the hard work and part-time scholarship of John Rylands. The manuscript section of the library has records inscribed on clay, bark, bamboo, parchment, papyrus and vellum. These date from 3000 BC to the present day, and there also more than 250,000 documents dating from between the eleventh and twentieth centuries. The building itself was purpose-built in 1900 and is a fine neo-Gothick example of the work of Basil Champneys.

The Central Library, in complete contrast, is a circular building constructed between 1930 and 1934 and is one of the finest reference libraries in Europe – we have certainly seen none better or more efficient. It also has a coffee house and a theatre in the basement. There is also another theatre which has been constructed within the Corn Exchange. We have seen many fine performances in the Royal Exchange Theatre which has been designed to allow the actors to perform 'in the round'.

The Town Hall, which is also open to the public, was built in 1876 and is a fine example of the work of Charles Waterhouse who also designed the South Kensington Natural History Museum in London. Inside there is a delightfully proportioned hall, the walls of which bear twelve local scenes painted by Ford Madox Brown. There is also a fine collection of civic plate. Outside are statues including John Bright, Richard Cobden, John Dalton and Sir Charles Hallé. The Hallé Orchestra dates from the Art Treasures Exhibition of 1857, and Sir Charles then began the Hallé concerts as a private venture which proved to be very successful. After his death the Hallé Concert Society was set up in 1898, and the Orchestra has had a worldwide reputation ever since. We wonder why Sir Charles is buried in Salford, but that city should always be carefully explored as it too has many treasures on offer.

The Rochdale Canal near Castlefields in Manchester.

Salford, although connected to Manchester by bridges over the Irwell and the docks, does have a separate and proudly defended individuality, and there is nothing wrong with this. After all, L S Lowrie was born here and the Salford Art Gallery has a comprehensive collection of his works, with the 'matchstick' figures which were his hallmark.

During the 1980s Liverpool's Pier Head was completely refurbished, and during the 1990s a similar facelift is being planned for the Salford Docks area; already the Salford Quays project is gathering momentum. We hope that there will be room for museums as good as that at Peel Park where there is a good collection of paintings plus Lark Hill Place, which is actually a reconstruction of a typical nineteenth-century Lancastrian street.

At Buile Hill Park is the science museum which depicts the once-extensive local coalmining industry, and there is also a strong natural history section. Salford has few really old buildings left, but Ordsall Hall, the medieval home of the Radcliffe family, has been restored and is open to the public. It is said, on pretty solid evidence, that it was the Radcliffes who brought Flemish weavers to Salford and thus established the textile tradition which still hangs on by the slimmest of threads. Local industry has had to diversify, but times continue to be hard.

Ordsall was built between the fourteenth and sixteenth centuries, and according to the Victorian novelist Harrison Ainsworth, Guy Fawkes visited the Hall and hatched the Gunpowder Plot beneath its roof. Try as we may, we find it impossible to turn up documentary proof of this event, so it may well be an example of Ainsworth's artistic licence. The moat which once surrounded the Hall has long gone and it now overlooks dockland. When we first visited Ordsall Hall in the 1950s it was almost derelict, but in 1960 Salford Corporation bought it and after many years of varying fortunes, it is now a spruce museum and cannot have looked better for two centuries. The Radcliffes would obviously not recognise modern Salford, but they would certainly be proud to find that their home has withstood so well the ravages of time.

Manchester, apart from its docks, which made it the third of

A day in the life of the Manchester Exchange in 1936. The Exchange Theatre is now constructed within this splendid building.

Britain's seaports, was fed by three canals – the Rochdale which is described in Chapter 4, the Bridgewater, and the Manchester Ship Canal.

It is often said that the Bridgewater was the first canal in Britain; actually the Sankey Brook was earlier but this is merely a cut inland from the Mersey. The Duke of Bridgewater's canal was the first inland canal and was initially designed to connect his coal mines at Worsley to the developing industries of Manchester five miles away. Carrying fuel by unreliable roads was expensive, and once the cut was opened, down went the price of coal and up went the profits. The young Duke was not so much a genius but more of an observant traveller, who saw the continental canals whilst on the Grand Tour which was then the obligatory journey for all young aristrocrats. Three men must take the credit for this canal – the Duke himself, his agent John Gilbert who was himself an able engineer but who knew the practical worth of James Brindley, who was all but illiterate. Gilbert, however, deserves most of the credit, and is seldom given any at all.

The Bill was applied for in 1759 and the canal finally reached Manchester in 1763. At the Worsley end the cut actually penetrated deep into the mine workings, the coal being floated out on boats which because of their crude but functional workmanship had wooden staves projecting at all angles like broken ribs. For this reason they were known as 'starvation boats'. One autumn morning we stood overlooking the mine entrance observing an old rotting hulk looking like a starvation boat and sticking out like raw spare-ribs from the blood-red water of the canal. This colour is caused by oxidising iron, surprisingly it is not poisonous, and we watched a young boy catching sticklebacks, frequently withdrawing his net to transfer his catch to a bucket, or to allow for the passage of a pleasure boat.

Originally it was intended to incorporate the Irwell into the canal system but in 1760 the Duke changed the plan to take the canal across the river and then run southwards to Manchester, thus keeping the route independent of unreliable river water. This involved the construction of a 39-foot-high, three-arched aqueduct at Barton, the first ever to be constructed in England, which was kept watertight by 'puddling' or trampling the lining

An engraving of Heaton in about 1830 showing James Wyatt's design at its best.

with clay. During the construction of the Manchester Ship Canal it was demolished and replaced by the unique Barton Swing Aqueduct which carries the Bridgewater Canal over the more modern Ship Canal.

Whilst this work was going on in 1890, an ancient dugout wooden canoe was unearthed and found to be perfectly preserved in the peaty oxygen-free soil. The Bridgewater Canal then passes through Stretford which is about ten miles from Worsley where there is a junction called Water's Meeting which allows traffic to Manchester to turn left, but there are also connections with the Ship Canal and with the Rochdale. The Bridgewater itself branches here with a link to Manchester going hard left, whilst the right turn heads through Cheshire to the Mersey, passing through Lymm, Stockton-Heath, Daresbury where Lewis Carrol, the author of *Alice in Wonderland* was born, Preston Brook and Runcorn.

Once the canal had reached its main objetive – Manchester – the Duke set about clearing the Castlefield area of the Roman town and building wharves and warehouses to recoup his money. It soon became obvious, however, that his other objective was to compete with the Mersey and Irwell Navigation Company and continue the canal, thus providing Manchester with a direct link to the sea. It could therefore become an inland port in direct competition with Liverpool. It almost succeeded. By 1800 a 6¼-mile branch canal was cut linking Worsley with Leigh and then on to meet the Leeds to Liverpool. In 1838 the three Hulme locks were constructed at Castlefield down to the Irwell, and as late as 1962 these were replaced by a single lock having a depth of 12 feet.

What Manchester really needed, however, was a more direct link with the sea and one which would take ocean-going ships. Then, and only then, could Liverpool be threatened. Thus the idea of the Manchester Ship Canal was born which, when it opened in 1894, fulfilled the dreams of eighteenth-century Manchester merchants jealous of the fortunes made by the Liverpool importers who could hold their inland rivals to ransom knowing that they had the monopoly on both imports and exports.

Politics and finance prevented any workable scheme being put forward until 1882, and even then work did not begin until 1887, but seven years later the cut was opened by Queen Victoria on 21st May 1894. She arrived on board the Admiralty yacht *Enchantress*. Not all went smoothly during the construction and the project would never have survived if Manchester Corporation had not realised its value and made up the financial shortfalls. The Ship Canal in its day must have been an enterprise similar to the Channel Tunnel of the 1990s.

The Ship Canal links Manchester with Liverpool some 42 miles away, and we have walked much of its towpath with friends who live at Irlam. They told us of the days when the canal was busy with ocean-going ships, some so heavily loaded that from their house they could sometimes hear the bumping and scraping noises as the keels touched the bottom of Britain's most impressive waterway. The canal meets the Mersey estuary at Eastham locks on the Cheshire side of the river. One thing is certain – it ensured that Manchester held its position as 'Cottonopolis' – but more recent events have reduced the importance of Manchester Docks and therefore the revenue from the canal.

All sorts of schemes have been suggested to make fresh use of the Manchester Ship Canal, and it was an integral part of Manchester's plans to host the Olympic Games. We hope that this initiative can be sustained and that Salford Quays, the

'The charge of the Fire Brigade – Salford, 1897'.

Docks and the Ship Canal can become sites for water sports and other leisure activities with some housing and offices. Indeed the whole scene created by what were once Lancashire's 'dark satanic mills' has changed rapidly during the 1980s and is set to accelerate through the 1990s. Once more Lancashire is set to become a greener and more pleasant land.

CHAPTER 3

Oldham and along the Medlock to Manchester

The V-shaped valley between Ashton-under-Lyne and Oldham was ground out around 10,000 years ago following the Ice Age.

Out of the millstone grit country around Bishop Park, some four miles to the north-east of Oldham, rises the River Medlock, which flows in a more or less southerly course for about ten miles before swinging westwards into the cities of Manchester and Salford where its murky waters join the equally grubby Irwell near Regents Bridge. Compared to 1890, we must admit that even if some over-critical environmentalists do not agree, the 1991 rivers are much cleaner. This is not due to deliberate battles against pollution, but because of the decline of the cotton industry.

The majority of Lancashire towns developed in a most haphazard manner with little if any planning. Ashton-under-Lyne is an exception to this rule, and the now large cotton-spinning centre was supervised during its development by the Lords of the Manor, the Earls of Stamford. In 1750 Ashton was no more than a village of four narrow streets and a church. Between 1758 and 1847, when it received its borough charter, the Earl insisted that his surveyors followed the American mid-west pattern and laid out streets meeting at right angles, thus producing a grid-iron plan.

The parish church of St. Michael, though restored during the nineteenth century, no doubt with money made from cotton spinning, dates from the thirteenth century and still has some excellent stained glass from around 1500. In the days when very few people could read or write, stained glass functioned as a visual aid and depicted biblical stories or the history of important local families. St. Michael's has both and there are five splendid windows telling of St. Helena and her discovery of the True Cross. Other glass tells of the Assheton family who still have an ancestral home at Downham where the owner, Lord Clitheroe, is an Assheton (see Chapter 10). There was also a branch at Middleton between Rochdale and Manchester.

32

Here is Oldham in the late 1940s, with the multi-storeyed spinning mills and their lodges which provided the essential water. Also clearly seen are the geometrical lines of terraced houses. Workers did not have far to travel to work in those days.

At Ashton-under-Lyne lived a real black sheep of the family, Sir Ralph, who was known as the Black Knight from the colour of his armour. Another Assheton, Sir Thomas, distinguished himself during the Wars of the Roses, especially at the Battle of Nevilles Cross at Durham.

There is no doubt that Oldham should be regarded as King Cotton's palace, at least as far as spinning was concerned. We never tire of wandering its streets, camera at the ready, notebook in constant use, and imagination running riot. We have seen scratches on the bedroom windows of terraced cottages made by the long poles of the 'knocker up' whose job it was to wake the workers in time for their shift at the mills before the days of the alarm clock. At the peak of production 145,000 people were employed in more than 250 mills, some of many storeys in which 18 million spindles clicked away making vast profits for businessmen who went to the Manchester Exchange twice a week to secure orders.

A good percentage of their profits were spent on the town. The Town Hall in Yorkshire street built in 1841 like a Greek temple was enlarged in 1880 to reflect Oldham's growing opulence. The art gallery deserves its reputation as one of the first outside an English city, and many of its pictures were given by Charles Lees in the closing years of the nineteenth century. Particularly notable are the watercolours of Cozens, Constable, Girtin, Prout, Cox and especially Constable and Turner.

Oldham's most famous son is probably Sir William Walton, whose father had a fine bass voice, and he was sent to the Manchester College of Music, which had been endowed by Charles Lees. Whenever we return from Oldham, or from the surprisingly green moorlands which surround it, we play some of Walton's music and wonder if his First Symphony or perhaps Belshazzar's Feast was at all inspired by the town and its setting. Nature creeps surprisingly close to the town, and there are two areas which we find particularly attractive. Situated high above Oldham and Saddleworth is the Chew Valley reservoir some 1600 feet (487.5 metres) above sea level, and therefore a little cold and exposed to be attractive to wildfowl. Any birds present will probably be resting rather than feeding and will soon move on. It is the moorland including Saddleworth Moor, however, which is of interest to both fell walkers and naturalists. The jagged crags and expanses of scree are home to mountain hare, introduced in the 1880s, and the native stoat and weasel with patches of heather and bilberry providing cover for birds.

From the A62 Oldham to Huddersfield road turn onto the B669 towards Grasscroft. Turn left for a short distance along the A670 and then sharp right to Greenfield. A track leads to Chew Valley where there is ample parking. In winter it should be remembered that these hills are dangerous when the snow lies thick and high winds can produce blizzards. Even in the warmer months a knowledge of the weather forecast is essential as many dangerous hazards can be concealed by low cloud.

Holden Clough is sited between Oldham and Ashton-under-Lyne close to Bardsley and at an altitude of 450 feet (136 metres). It runs in an easterly direction for about 1¼ miles (2km) and a tributary stream of the River Medlock runs through it. The total area is 36 acres (14.5 hectares), of which just over 26 acres (10.5 hectares) make up the nature reserve. Adjoining the reserve is a pond which adds to the diversity of the wildlife. In 1861 the Oldham, Ashton and Guide Bridge Railway was thrust through the area and a culvert was made to channel the stream beneath. The railway was closed in 1965 and a housing estate was built at about the same time along the boundary of the clough. Despite these disturbances Holden Clough continues to fascinate naturalists who believe that it contains relict fauna and flora which once occupied the whole of the now mainly industrialised area. In 1965 the trustees of the estate of the seventh Earl of Stanford and Warrington allowed the clough to be administered by the North Western Naturalists' Union who, along with other bodies and individuals, have compiled an impressive list of its fauna and flora. Geologically the area is fascinating, consisting of deposits of sand, gravel and sandy clay with occasional bands of peat. 'Foreign' rocks or 'erratics' carried by ice from the Borrowdale volcanic area in the Lake District also occur.

Almost a hundred species of bird have been recorded, more than forty of which breed, most being concentrated at the eastern area of the reserve where there are more trees. The fields along the northern edge provide feeding for lapwing, golden plover and great and lesser black backed gulls as well as herring, common (in cold winters) and black headed gulls. Redwings with fieldfare feed in winter on the hawthorn trees and goldfinches on the dry thistle seeds. A number of small ponds fringed with reeds attract snipe and moorhen throughout the year, and in summer swallows and martins hunt for insects. Bardsley is directly on the A627 from Oldham to Ashton-under-Lyne. Access points to the reserve are close to old railway line.

By far the best way to understand this part of Lancashire is to follow the River Medlock from its source to its junction with the Irwell in Manchester.

What a Jekyll and Hyde river the Medlock still is; how it has survived years of pollution prior to recent improvements is one of the great miracles of river history. In 1890, for example, the farmers around Littlemoss appealed for a supply of clean water for their cattle, as the Industrial Revolution and population increase reached a suffocating peak. The Medlock's water was in demand to power machines, and all that it received in return was an ever-increasing volume of waste materials spewed into the drains to mix with the untreated sewage issuing from the over-crowded houses. At Woodhouses by the banks of a tributary stream called Lord's Brook there was once a building called a Bowk house in which yarn was prepared for weaving. A stinking mixture of greasy oil, lye (which was made from urine collected each morning from local houses) and wood ash was used to treat the yarn. Fatty globules left the Bowk house and floated downstream to join the Medlock, making its contribution to an unsavoury soup, along with the blood from slaughter houses, which were usually sited as close as possible to a watercourse.

Small wonder that folk began to complain about the stench, and many were even more worried that over-adventurous children playing along the banks of the river were in real danger. The problem for the children of Ardwick was pointed out in the *Manchester City News* of January 7th 1939 by a lady boasting the name of Councillor Nellie Beer! She pointed out that a surprisingly attractive looking bed of sand in the river was a fatal attraction.

As building went on around and often actually over the rivers of Manchester, the demand for space and also their filthy state meant an instant pressure on the local authorities to sanction river straightening and culverting programmes. Even as late as 1959 it was agreed that the great winding loop – in its past a crystal-clear meander full of trout – from Downing Street to a point near Upper Brook Street was to be straightened out to make room for extensions to the College of Science and Technology and also for a new road to bypass the city centre plus an associated 1,200 yard (1107 metres) flyover. A massive culvert over the Medlock was an integral part of this scheme. This has now been completed, and the river has disappeared for ever from the daylight which once gave it life.

On October 5th 1961 the *Manchester Evening News* reported yet another straightening-out of the River Medlock – this time at Clayton Vale. The idea was 'to give the corporation a greater area for tipping operations which in turn will be laid out as playing fields . . . the total cost of realignment will be £286,000

The interior of a cotton-spinning mill.

which is £110,000 cheaper than culverting the present stretch of the river through the vale'. All this frenzied activity must have reduced the once abundant wildlife almost to extinction but there were – and still are – silver linings to the storm clouds which had long been gathering over the Medlock. One such glimmer of hope was the tale of 'Glug', the 7-inch (17.5 cm) long carp which in 1965 was found alive – but only just kicking – in a muddy pool beneath yet another culvert in the process of construction. The workman who named it 'Glug' thought it had been washed from the temporarily diverted course of the Medlock during a heavy period of rain the previous week. The reporter of this event made the point that only rats and newts were able to survive at this point due to chemical and sewage pollution. We can easily understand the presence of rats, but how newts could ever survive here is beyond us. Rats will actually eat sewage, and on one occasion on the Medlock we observed an animal chomping away at ice!

It is quite obvious from this brief account of the state of the Medlock Valley that the river was in desperate need of a clean-up, and the first glimmer of hope appeared in January 1968, when it was reported in the *Manchester Evening News* that plans were afoot to make the valley greener. 'Architects from Lancashire County Council and Oldham are working on plans to redevelop long stretches on the five mile long Medlock valley.' It took another couple of years for these plans to be formalised and they were to say the least, ambitious. A sports centre of what was described as 'sub-regional significance' was planned for Clayton Bridge, whilst at Medlock Vale, an intensive recreational complex was to include bowling alleys, dance halls, a pub, a restaurant, a golf driving range and what was described as a fun palace. Moorside at Droylesden was to have an equestrian centre to be linked by a bridle path to the river valley. At Ashton Moss a garden centre was envisaged, with a commercially operated tree nursery, whilst money was to be allotted to develop the existing playing fields. Glodwick was to have an artifical ski-run, adventure playground and a zoo. Lees was to have riverside paths, parkland and as complete a facelift as was possible in such an industrialised area, which required what the planners called 'residential infill'. As usual these plans only raised local hopes which were then gradually disappointed, and there is the bitter suggestion that had the Medlock Valley been a tributary of the Thames, the money would have been found very quickly.

The reservoirs at Strinesdale were considered ideal for development as a sailing, fishing and walking centre, whilst there would also be ample space left for wildlife. Daisy Nook, which has always been something of a beauty spot – a sort of lung for the hard-working cotton operatives – was to continue as an informal park, and among the planned amenities were boating, fishing, miniature golf and a camp site. The Ashton Canal was also to be given a facelift. The area around Bardsley and Park Bridge was to be converted into a picnic site, although its peace was not guaranteed as motor cycling was to be encouraged. Holden Clough, described earlier in this chapter, was to be incorporated into the scheme, and the whole enterprise was to be supervised from a visitors' centre at Park Bridge.

Local newspapers and radio stations in all towns and cities thrive on reporting such schemes which seldom, if ever, get off the drawing board, although the 'planners' often earn a good living from their undoubted skill in generating expectations. With local government reorganisation coming in 1974 the Greater Manchester Council, the Metropolitan Borough of Oldham and Tameside got together with the North West Water Authority, now privatised but still keen to promote a green and caring image, and things have started to happen. In some areas improvements have been slow to come, but in others the only suitable word to describe the progress is dramatic. The best way to understand what has happened – and what is still happening – to the river is to follow the well-marked Medlock Trail from the hills in which it is born right into the heart of the city. A leaflet produced by the GMC put the importance of the river in a nutshell, describing it as a 'long green dagger thrusting into the heart of the city'.

Strinesdale is a wildfowl refuge, but the focus of attention in the Medlock Valley has been Daisy Nook where the Easter Fair has been held for more than 200 years, its only problem being its over-use. In 1976, 85 acres were set aside as a Country Park, paths were laid out, ecologically delicate areas were protected and good parking was provided. Local schools were involved in tree-planting schemes and the presence of so many people – often up to 4,000 on Sunday afternoons – keeps vandalism within bounds. Sections of the Ashton Canal, built originally for the use of mills and mines, have been adapted as water amenities whilst other derelict bits have been filled in and serve as bridleways. Looking down from the canal, you can see the

Medlock meandering along its valley, appearing surprisingly unaffected from this angle by the years of human interference.

Crime Lake – what a curious name – was formed as a result of a landslip blocking a culvert, after which the resourceful Victorians made full use of its potential. A local entrepreneur operated the *Pioneer*, a small steamer which ferried passengers between Failsworth and Oldham Road, picking up passengers at Crime Lake, which was then usually bulging with visitors to its tearooms and fairground. Rowing boats could also be hired, and these remain to the present day, but the steamer has long gone, much to the benefit of an assortment of wildfowl including Canada geese, tufted duck, pochard, mallard and the occasional great-crested grebe and dabchick.

At Clayton Vale around 100 acres have been reclaimed from old rubbish tips, and a network of footpaths, liberally provided with seats plus thousands of skilfully planted trees – many native species sensibly included – are becoming a welcome focus for an increasing number of daytrippers. It may, however, take the best part of a generation for folk to realise that the rubbish tip has gone.

The warden service is based at Park Bridge and although this spot is far from being beautiful, it does typify the Medlock as a working river. Two hundred years ago Park Bridge was a hard-working village based on Samuel Lees's ironworks which had been established in the 1780s. Fuel for the blast furnaces came from coalmines which were conveniently close, and cheap transport was provided by an often bewildering network of canal branches which to modern observers appear to be going nowhere. The village, signposted off the A627 road, is typified by rows of terraced houses plus a church and an institute, all of which were illuminated by gas produced locally.

Whilst the Medlock itself is recovering with a lot of help from its friends, the same cannot be said about some of its tributaries which are now lost for ever. Who, for example, has never heard of the Tib, Shooters Brook or the Cornbrook? A few references to the *Manchester Evening News* of October 19th 1934 may help visitors to present-day Manchester to at least walk the route taken by these streams: 'The River Tib was the first of the Manchester rivers to disappear from view. Manchester people decided nearly 150 years ago that they had seen quite

The crowds enjoying the Medlock at Daisy Nook on Easter Monday.

enough of it, and they began to cover it over with flags.'

Gradually the whole length of the Tib has been covered over from the hillside on Oldham Road to its junction with the Medlock near where the old Gaythorn gasworks once stood. The approximate course of the river can be followed along Tib Street itself, then close to Market Street, after which it has been diverted underground around the Town Hall and the Central Reference Library to Oxford Road and then into the Medlock. What a way to treat an English trout stream!

Shooters Brook has its source around Monsall Road and is culverted beneath the crowded industrial suburb of Ancoats and what was once called London Road Railway Station but is now called Piccadilly. The only indication of its presence is in the name of Brook Street in the Princess Street area of the city close to which it too feeds the Medlock. When it was a country stream it was famous for its snipe shooting. This was organised from Garratt Hall which stood for a long time after being swallowed by the city area of Granby Row and Whitworth Street. There is still an hotel in this area called the Old Garratt.

The Cornbrook is the most substantial of the hidden rivers, and it runs from Gorton right under the city and now emerges in the Pamona Dockland area where its waters help to maintain the water levels of the Manchester Ship Canal. In Hulme it passes beneath the Bridgewater Canal and there is a clever device in the bowels of the earth which in times of water shortage can divert supplies into this canal.

This is what we find so exciting about Old Lancashire. There are so many hidden faces to prove that even in the areas where the Industrial Revolution hit hardest, echoes of the countryside can still be found by those prepared to give of their time.

CHAPTER 4

Around Rochdale

A good way to explore any town is to follow the route of the old turnpike roads which were built to feed the heart of the settlement; in other cases following the line of a canal can be just as effective.

To reach Rochdale we followed the road from Todmorden to the Old Toll House at Steanor Bottom which stands almost on the border between Lancashire and Yorkshire. Down in the valley bottom runs the Rochdale Canal. Prior to the seventeenth century the roads were appalling and each town or parish was required to maintain its own highways which it usually did by filling in holes with stone and rubble. This dates to the Statute of Winchester of 1285, affirming manorial responsibility for maintaining the King's Highways. Some erosion of responsibilities took place at the time of the dissolution of the monasteries.

The idea of turnpikes requiring tolls to be paid for the upkeep of the roads began in 1663 with the essential road from London to Scotland via York which ran close to the line of the present A1. Obviously the textile industries of northern England greatly benefited from improved transportation, the increased profits allowed the mills to grow larger, and the lower and more competitive prices stimulated demand. Steanor Bottom toll bar did a roaring trade in the mid-eighteenth century.

The Toll House has been accurately restored and it is possible to read the toll board, from which it can be seen that the prices, compared to the average weekly wage at the time, were quite high. Toll houses were usually set at road junctions and with their windows set to enable the collector of the tolls to have a clear view of both highways. The keepers of both roads and canal houses were usually ex-soldiers or sailors whose discipline proved ideal, and they were in plentiful supply as the Napoleonic Wars came to an end after the battle of Waterloo in 1815.

The Coach House at Littleborough just beyond Steanor Bottom is a fine Grade 2 listed building recently restored by a locally run committee. Entry is free and there is an excellent little cafe as clean as a pin and overflowing with friendliness. The locals are able to hire the building for conferences, parties and weddings. There is a permanent exhibition of local art on view, much of it for sale. In warmer weather a door is opened from the cafe onto a patio. All this has been achieved without destroying the feeling of history. The paved square sandwiched between the Falcon Inn, the coach house which it once served, and Holy Trinity church must have been a hive of activity as the coaches changed horses and the inn fed the travellers.

Littleborough was on the main route between Lancashire and Yorkshire over Blackstone Edge and via Todmorden to the mill towns of Burnley and Blackburn. The little town itself is now no more than a suburb of Rochdale (more's the pity), although its population exceeds 13,000. The Coach House is an ideal situation from which to explore many other exciting places such as Blackstone Edge and Hollingworth Lake.

There was a Roman road which ran over the moors from Manchester to Ilkley although the greater part of it has long been overgrown and lost. At Blackstone Edge, however, a long stretch over the high moorland is in a fine state of preservation, and even the foundations remain. There is a groove running down the centre of the road which has caused a great deal of argument among archaeologists. Some think it was turfed in order to allow the horses to get a grip and others have stated, without any evidence, that the groove was worn by chariots. Others feel that it may not even be Roman at all but if not, then what is it? The road is crossed by the Pennine Way. There is a fine walk from the Coach House up onto the Edge and also to Hollingworth Lake.

Hollingworth Lake Country Park is overlooked by the M62, the modern-day trans-Pennine route. There is a well-appointed visitors centre with toilets, bookshop, cafe and information centre. There are good facilities for children and for the disabled. A wheelchair is available for hire, and there are a number of spacious tree-lined car parks.

Hollingworth is not a natural lake but a compensation reservoir of 120 acres constructed to supply the Rochdale

The Littleborough Coach House.

Canal. At the present time it still supplies the surrounding area of canal with up to two million gallons a day, but it now enjoys a central role within the Country Park. In Victorian times the lake was much appreciated by the hard-working mill hands who used it as a leisure area situated above the then smokey town of Rochdale. The Country Park was opened in 1974 and since that time has gone from strength to strength. The visitor centre features an excellent tape/slide show presenting the history and natural history of the area, but anyone with a couple of hours to spare and the stamina to cover 2½ miles will find the circular nature trail surprisingly rich.

From the area of Hollingworth, the bulk of Blackstone Edge can be seen rising to a height of around 1550 feet (472 metres). Close to the lake is the Fish Inn and several marshy areas in which grow water mint, yellow iris, water forget-me-not and ragged robin.

The footpath follows the line of an old road, and approaches a one-time toll gate close to which is a metal sign which has been restored and provides a feeling of history which increases

Plaque on wall of Littleborough Coach House.

as one approaches the hamlet of Hollingworth Fold. This must have been even more isolated before the reservoir was built. In the nineteenth century it had a workhouse, a small school and its own public house called The Mermaid.

The nature trail then earns its name by entering an area of marshland which provides a refuge for a wide variety of birds, insects and plants. Here are found breeding great crested grebe, coot, snipe and mallard. Other species breeding here include reed bunting, willow warbler and moorhen. We often visit the area in winter when the birds usually outnumber the people.

The trail then passes an area known as The Promontory, which in Victorian times was known as the 'Weavers' Seaport'. This should not be thought derogatory, and when viewed in May and June with rhododendron blooming, it really is beautiful. The Victorians certainly knew how to enjoy themselves, and a paddle steamer which operated on the lake was often full to overflowing during the warmer months. Fortunately modern visitors can still enjoy a short trip on the *Lady Alice*, a comfortable motor cruiser.

Just before The Promontory we always pay a visit to the bird hide overlooking the nature reserve, and in spring we have watched a young great crested grebe, still looking pale in its juvenile plumage, there being no sign of its parents, but its presence was sure proof that one of Britain's shyest birds can breed close to a busy recreation area providing space is set aside for it.

As we reached The Promontory, the cafe was doing a roaring trade, yachts were taking advantage of a gentle breeze and anglers were catching their share of perch, pike and roach. The *Lady Alice* landed a happy crop of visitors, and children's laughter echoed from the playground above the rhododendrons. As the sun came out after a rather dull morning, the temperature rose dramatically and the dogs, whilst kept on leads most of the time, found quiet areas to swim and drink. It is good to see them made welcome, and outside the toilets at the visitor centre there are rings to which they can be tied whilst their owners are otherwise engaged.

One reason why the Hollingworth area is so popular is that there are seats all the way round, all tastes and ages are catered for and refreshments can be obtained at several points. Bar snacks are available at the Queens Hotel, and just beyond this is a Blackpool-like amusement centre, a boating club and a place where owners can obtain permission to launch their own craft. It is also possible to hire small boats. The final stretch of the circuit passes the dams of the reservoir and reaches the Fish

Hotel, another establishment catering well for the hungry and thirsty, and a further short walk returns us to the visitor centre. For those who prefer a wilder treck, a really splendid footpath leads through fields alongside rippling brooks and over well-contructed stiles back to Littleborough. Surely no Country Park can offer such variety as Hollingworth. The 'Weavers' Seaport' has still not lost its nautical air, and yet careful and sensible management has resulted in an area very rich in wildlife, a feature which is becoming more obvious as the years go by – a perfect balance between leisure, history and natural history.

The same three features are also typical of the Rochdale Canal, easily explored from Hollingworth Country Park by following the feeder cut carrying water to the main canal.

The Rochdale Canal was a brave enterprise completed in 1804, and its 33-mile length climbed up, over and down the Pennines and required no fewer than 92 locks. Its importance was that it ran from Castlefield in Manchester to Sowerby Bridge, thus linking with the Mersey at the Lancashhire end and with the Calder and Hebble Navigation at the Yorkshire end. At the Manchester end there were important links with both the Ashton Canal and with the Bridgewater. The towpath can still be walked, although the last commercial boat used the canal in 1937. The Rochdale was not even thought important enough to be included in the nationalisation scheme of 1948. In 1952 the canal was officially abandoned and this was confirmed by an Act of Parliament, but some sections are being lovingly restored by members of the hard-working Rochdale Canal Preservation Society. This was one of three trans-Pennine routes, and its summit was between Rochdale and Littleborough, with the highest flight of locks situated just behind The Summit public house. It is hereabouts that canal engineering reached a peak, John Rennie being the surveyor, but the work was supervised by William Jessop.

When Rochdale is mentioned, folk think of Gracie Fields, Cyril Smith and cotton, but initially Rochdale, set around 400 feet (146 metres) up on the Pennine moors was very much dependent on wool. As with Oldham, there was settlement on these moors in the Bronze Age, and the local museum has a fine collection of flints. In Saxon times, Rochdale was a village under the control of Athelstan, the West Saxon monarch. It is

Healy Dell Viaduct – The trains have gone and it now carries sewage and tourists.

mentioned in the Domesday Book and was one of the largest manors within the hundred of Salford. The market charter was granted in 1251 and its prosperity was still based on wool until towards the end of the eighteenth century when cotton became dominant.

The relationship between mill owners and their operatives was not always amicable and one of the main areas of argument was the payment of part of the workers' wages in kind. This took the form of providing often sub-standard food from the factory-owned shop. It was in Rochdale that workers finally decided to set up their own co-operative store, the building now being one of the most unique museums in the country.

We can remember being sent to our local co-op with a list of shopping and clutching a red ten-shilling note and the 'divi-book'. In this was entered the total amount of money spent, and periodically this was added up and a dividend was paid – there were always extra sweets to look forward to on divi-day, especially in the period following the ending of rationing. What fun it was to watch real grocers at work before everything arrived pre-packed. They could remove a pound of butter from a barrel and pat it flat between a couple of flat wooden spatulas. We never knew them to spill even a grain of sugar when transferring it from large sacks to small blue paper bags. They could cut bacon to precise instructions. There always seemed to be a queue but no one seemed to mind. Perhaps it was because of the delightfully varied smells of cases of open tea, bacon, apples, soap, coffee being ground, candles, bleach and pipe tobacco.

Because of these memories we can never resist a visit to the Rochdale Pioneers Museum in Toad Lane, just behind the main shopping centre on Hunters Lane. The Society, formed on 21st December 1844, was the first successful attempt at co-operative buying, and in 1931 the Co-operative Union bought the shop as a museum. Between 1974 and 1978 the museum was closed and given a thorough overhaul, and it has now been restored to its original condition. No-one interested in the social history of Lancashire can afford to miss a stroll down Toad Lane. There is a shop selling postcards, books, tea towels and the history of the Co-operative movement. We just wish

Bacup Station – also now closed.

there was someone there to pat butter, cut bars of soap, grind coffee and cut bacon.

Rochdale also has its share of fine buildings including the Gothick-style Town Hall designed by W.H. Crossland and opened in 1871. The frontage stretches for 264 feet (80 metres), whilst inside is a hammerbeam roof and a fresco painted by Henry Holiday depicting 'The signing of Magna Carta'. Rochdale thus has its Town Hall which is a monument to the creation of wealth, and the Co-op, a tribute to the poor fighting to make ends meet. The town also had its famous sons and daughter, and in addition to those already mentioned we must list John Bright and John Collier. Bright was born in 1811 and achieved fame because of his efforts to repeal the Corn Laws; there is a bronze statue of him in Hillside Gardens. John Collier was best known under the name of Tim Bobbin, and he was the first of the Lancashire dialect poets. Collier was born at Urmston near Manchester in 1708 but in 1729 he became schoolmaster at Milnrow, then a woollen handloom weaving village on the outskirts of Rochdale which is now dominated by the trans-Pennine M62 motorway. John, or should we call him Tim, remained at Milnrow until his death in 1786, but his life was not at all happy and he drank rather more than was good for him, making the extra cash necessary by selling his dialect verse and painting pub signs. There is an inn in Milnrow named after him and another Tim Bobbin between Burnley and Padiham. Some of John Collier's original work is held in Rochdale's Central Library where it is also worth seeing the Ember collection of cricket memorabilia. We often wonder what the Ember collection and the Ashes have in common if our readers will excuse the pun!

Rochdale is surrounded by several settlements including Heywood, Wardle, Newhey, and Middleton which the local town guide describes as the link between Rochdale and Manchester. Some old locals still refer to natives as Moonrakers, a name which arose from the time when poachers threw their bag of game into a pond as their pursuers closed in on them. They explained their interest in the pond by pointing to a reflection of the moon in the water and saying they were trying to rake in a cheese!

Middleton has a modern centre, but its lineage is as old as that of Rochdale, with the half-timbered Ye Olde Boars Head dating back to the sixteenth century, but there has apparently been a building on the site from the eleventh century. It was at one time used as a court room and a jail.

St Leonard's Church was built in 1524, but incorporates stone from an earlier Norman foundation. The present church was built by Sir Richard Assheton, Lord of the Manor of Middleton who, with his local archers, did much to defeat the Scots at the Battle of Flodden in 1513. In the church is a stained-glass window commemorating these archers, and thus we have one of the oldest war memorials in England.

Another road out of Rochdale leads to Bacup; at one time a railway connected the two, and part of this line is now a nature reserve.

Healey Dell is part of the valley of the River Spodden between Rochdale and Bacup and was once the home of fat trout, healthy otters and pine martens, two mammals now long gone. It also has rich folklore. One of the springs feeding the Spodden is still called Robin Hood's Well. It is said that way back in the twelfth century a witch cast a spell on the young

Horse buses like this on Cheatham Street, Rochdale were a feature of the developing mill towns.

Earl of Huntington who was staying at Healey Hall. Her spell lured Robin to the well, where she pretended to be his old nursemaid. She told him that he would never inherit his Earldom without her magic ring to prove his identity. The witch persuaded him to gaze into the magic well and the poor gullible lad got such a shock that he fainted. Then the witch flew away on her broomstick, giving her black cat a lift as she went. The King of the Fairies, however, emerged from his chapel and gave Robin his own magic ring which he told him to take to the witches' coven high up in the Dell and to interrupt them whilst they were hatching a spell against him. When Robin threw the ring into the couldron as instructed, there was a blinding flash and the witches were reduced to tiny evil-looking fairies confined for ever to the Fairy chapel. If you look down into the 'chapel' and at the gurgling waters, it is easy to see how the legend arose — the eroded rocks do indeed resemble grotesque faces!

Another of the many unproven stories relating to the Dell is about Lord Byron, who is said to have visited relations who were Lords of the Manor of Rochdale. On a visit to the Dell with a lady love he was inspired to sit down and compose a poem. If this is just speculation, there can be no doubt whatever that the local dialect writer Edwin Waugh loved and wrote a great deal about the Dell. His character, Besom Ben, travelled from Rochdale through what is easily recognised as Healey Dell with its old well and mill.

The human impact on the Dell was minimal until the construction of the Rochdale to Bacup branch railway line, which was built by the Lancashire and Yorkshire Railway Company towards the end of the nineteenth century. It was never a real commercial success, and it is hardly surprising that it fell victim to the Beeching cuts of the 1960s. There was never any suggestions that it could or indeed should be saved as a going concern, but part of the route now forms part of the Healey Dell Nature Reserve opened in 1972 and funded by the County Borough of Rochdale and the Urban District of Whitworth. Two things saved the magnificent viaduct spanning the River Spodden – the nature trail and the fact that it now carries the main sewage pipe between Whitworth and Rochdale. The latter is, thankfully, unobtrusive.

Healey Dell is a recent name for an area which was once called Healey Dean, and way back in Anglo-Saxon times it was called Healey Thrutch – 'thrutch' meaning a cutting eroded through rocks by a river. It is highly likely that the fast-moving river hereabouts would have driven a corn mill. Experts agree that the course of the Spodden has changed little, if at all, since Saxon times; the oak and birch woodland on the north bank is a small section of a prehistoric forest, and there aren't many of these left in England.

Other parts of the Dell have been affected by the activities of the owners of Healey Hall which has been a landmark since medieval times. John de Heleya, who owned the hall in the thirteenth century, gave his name to the area. The present buildings date to the eighteenth century and the remains of old mill lodges make ideal habitats for moorhen, mallard and reed bunting. The presence of imported trees, especially hornbeam, suggests that the early mill owners were very conservation-

Steanor Bottom Toll House on the Lancashire/Yorkshire border.

minded. In Anglo-Saxon, 'horn' means hard and 'beam' means a tree, and so here we have a tree producing the hard timber ideal for the manufacture of cogwheels for mill machinery.

During the 1939-45 war the area was used as a store for high explosives, and when the temporary buildings fell into decay, the concrete and mortar provided a supply of lime ideal for the growth of plants such as ferns and orchids. The same situation applies along the old railway line. The remains of the old platforms at Shawclough and Broadley can still be seen, and it is easy to close your eyes and imagine steam engines puffing along. Because it was single track, the drivers loved this route, and it is reported by Allan Marshall in his splendid little book *Healey Dell* that the crew often stopped to remove the rabbits from snares set on previous trips. The station staff also had a more relaxed life than present-day railmen and spent time and effort cultivating the station gardens; regular competitions were held to find the most colourful. Among the ruins of Broadley station it is possible to find rhododendron, azalea and raspberries which grow wild among the native hawthorn and dog rose. Ferns grow in profusion on the platform, bridges and viaduct. This was built in 1867 of local sandstone and towers 105 feet (32 metres) over the Spodden; it is over 200 yards long and is supported by eight graceful arches. This is a remarkable feat of engineering and another example of Victorian skill and perseverance which are seen in the way that the steep gradient is surmounted. From Whitworth station to Britannia at Bacup – a distance of just over seven miles – the railway climbed more than 500 feet. There were continual problems with landslips, and just beyond the viaduct there are two bridges side by side, the second constructed when the land collapsed beneath the first. We wonder what the Irish navvies felt as they built the line above the valley so rich in stories about the 'little people'. We also wonder what the superstitious folk living in the valley felt in the early days of the railway, when the night trains spat fire and smoke into the darkness – how spooky it must have seemed.

These days it is almost as spooky to stand on the viaduct at dusk and listen to the haunting calls of tawny owls and imagine yourself waiting at Broadley station for a ghostly train to hoot loudly and come steaming and sparking out of the night.

CHAPTER 5

Following the Irwell

Few, if any, rivers have been so much maligned as the Irwell, and it was once said that anyone falling into its flood waters would dissolve before he drowned. These days Irwell country is improving fast and the Irwell valley towns are cleaner, the museums as good as any in the county, and it even has its own steam railway affectionately know as the Irwell Express. We always prefer to approach the Irwell from Burnley along the A671, passing the Deerplay Inn.

Standing at a height of 1326 feet (404 metres), the Deerplay is said to be the sixth highest inn in England, and in winter it feels exposed but bracing. A strong wind howled off the moors and drove icy lumps of hail into our faces. The black labrador shook his head every few minutes to remove the hail from his ears. We had followed the main road in the direction of Burnley, passing a war memorial perched on a hill and then looking down to the left at a doubleline of stonewalling. For many years we wondered why anyone should build two walls so close together until we walked between them accompanied by local historian Titus Thornber. He pointed out that this was the line of the old turnpike road connecting Burnley with Bacup. The walls were to prevent livestock from the fields wandering onto the road carrying fast-moving coaches. Titus showed us a number of 'pull ins' where coaches could pass, an old milestone, a series of huge stone slabs laid to culvert a stream and a horse trough almost hidden by grass and reeds. We dug our feet into the wet grass and crunched against the cobbles of the old road.

The Deerplay Inn itself was set on the turnpike and served the traveller well. The road branches at the Deerplay, the modern highway bearing left whilst the Old Turnpike winds its way to the right and, although narrow, it is still open. At one time the Deerplay stood on the opposite side of the road but when this was demolished, two cottages were converted into the New Deerplay which has been in existence for some 200 years.

It is said that Dick Turpin the infamous highwayman had relatives who lived here,and apparently he visited them several times. The spot is still pretty isolated and is often the first in the area to be cut off by the winter snows.

This is the only Inn to bear the name of Deerplay and obviously relates to the days when red and roe deer roamed the Forest of Rossendale and were no doubt hunted in the days when the Saxons and then the Normans held sway over this remote area. The hunting tradition is still maintained and the Holcombe Hunt occasionally chase hare over the local moorlands.

Beyond the Deerplay a footpath leads up to Thieveley Pike, passing en route the source of the Irwell. This stream must once have been a clear trout stream and was certainly one of the most popular rivers for otters – but with the Industrial Revolution it was polluted from its source to its confluence with the River Mersey around Manchester. Just behind Irwell House is the source of the river which consists only of a small pool of dark water, covered by a couple of flat stones but which never seems to run dry, even in long hot summers. In the nineteenth century when coal mining went on around the source, the river became so polluted that the Irwell was dead long before it reached Bacup, and although these mines have long since closed, there are still problems. The water is often stained rusty red with iron oxide seeping from the old workings – it has certainly made a nonsense of the Anglo-Saxon word 'Irwell', which is thought by some to translate as 'White Spring', although we favour another translation which means the Dark River.

At least the moorland landscape has recovered its beauty, and on one lovely day in early spring we followed the circular path from the Deerplay. A lark sang high above and the movement of the labrador through the heather flushed first a group of twite, and then a splendid merlin, both of which are rare but typical of this area.

The Irwell runs down into the little town of Bacup, a product of the Industrial Revolution which has suffered more from mill closures than almost any other town in Lancashire. We know and love it well, having lectured to and been members of the 'Bacup Nats' who have their headquarters in a

The Deerplay Inn, 1900.

building which was first a pub and then a doss house on
Yorkshire Street. The Nats, short for naturalists, were formed
in the 1870s by a group of mill workers who used Sunday –
their only completely free day – to wander the local moors,
whilst they learned the scientific names of the fauna and flora
from books propped up on their looms. Ever since this time
they have been collecting specimens and artefacts. As mills,
mines and railway lines closed, the collection just grew and
grew and is still growing. Every room bulges with excitingly
disorganised treasure: old dentists' instruments next to gas
masks, a miner's lamp near a set of antlers; tucked away in an
old outhouse is a working loom; and one long room has been
set out as a lecture theatre. The museum opens on Thursday
evenings and on Saturdays whilst visits at other times can be
arranged by appointment. They also brew a good cup of tea!

It was something of a tradition herebouts to set up scientific
and historical societies with organised visits using the
developing railway network. Bolton, Bury, Rochdale and
Oldham all had much-respected establishments, and there is
still a hotel in Prestwich called The Railway and Naturalist. We
often wonder what happened to their collection, but also we
shall never know.

Bacup is best visited during Easter weekend when its famous troup of Morris dancers, who wear clogs, clatter their way through the streets. They are known as the Coconut Dancers as they wear the husks of the coconut strapped to their knees and they also black their faces. They maintain that the correct name should be the Moorish, not Morris, dancers as the ritual goes back to the Crusades, hence their darkened faces. Whatever their origins, they are 'reet good fun'.

It is sad to see the decline in some of the mills although some have been converted to serve the needs of the shoe – or more particularly the slipper-industry. Stone cleaning is now well in evidence. The 'Nats' have supervised the garden area opposite the health centre which features some of the old street signs. Old Bacup can still be found on Saturdays when the market is in full swing. We know of very few other places where we can get a dish of black peas and a good helping of tripe and onions. The tourists potential of Bacup as an old Lancashire mill town has been realised just in time, and the 1990s will see many of its municipal, ecclesiastical and industrial buildings sensibly restored. One area to be left well alone is Elgin Street which, at only 17 feet long is the world's shortest street, and contains only one house.

The Irwell flows down a narrow valley from Bacup, culverted for a substantial part of the route, and until the water was 'managed', the town frequently flooded. We once made a television film on the River Irwell during which we walked along the old bank now beneath the road. How well we remember the face of an astonished young man gazing down into a metalled grate, wondering where the sound was coming from!

At Rawtenstall the Irwell is joined by Limey Water, a substantial tributary rising in the moorland above Crawshawbooth, a village which straddles the A56 road between Manchester and Burnley. This looks to be a small Victorian mill village, but four buildings should persuade visitors to halt awhile, although none are regularly open to the public. Swinshaw Hall is said to mark the spot the last wild boar in England was killed. Some historians, on tenuous evidence we must admit, say that the story of this hunt is described in the late fourteenth century tale of Sir Gawain and the Green

The Bacup Coconut Morris (or should it be Moorish?) dancers.

Knight. Whether this applies equally to other areas we do not feel qualified to say, but there is no doubt that much of the story reads very like Lancashire dialect. The rebuilt hall is now a nursing home for the elderly and is set high above the modern road, as is Goodshaw Chapel. This is a recently restored Baptist chapel dating to 1760. An even earlier religious house is set on the opposite side of the road close to the banks of Limey Water. This is the Quaker Meeting House built in 1716 which has a chair once used by George Fox himself. With the busy road close by it takes a little imagination to see the meeting house as having once been in a remote area overlooking a packhorse bridge leading onto the ancient road over the moors. As at most Meeting Houses, there were stables provided for those Friends who had travelled long distances to attend the often illegal services. It always pleases us to walk over the bridge and pass the cemetery where many local vets and pet lovers provide a peaceful end for their animals. The oldest building in Crawshawbooth is the Hall, now an Anglican conference centre, which has some splendid Tudor carvings of dark oak.

Anyone wishing to discover the history of Rossendale should visit the museum in Whitaker Park which is open free of charge every day from 1 pm to 5 pm. It was once called Oak Hill House, and built in 1840 for the Hardman family who owned Newhallhey Mill. There are displays of toll boards from the turnpike roads as well as a natural history collection. In 1990 a Victorian drawing room was set up and there is also a lot of information on the Irwell Valley industries.

The area between Rawtenstall and Bury is best explored by taking the steam train, but Rawtenstall itself can be seen laid out like a map from the path up to Waugh's Well which was restored in the 1980s and named after the dialect writer Edwin Waugh.

Many steam railways are purely tourist attractions routed through idyllic countryside but the 'Red Rose Line' running out of Bury's Bolton Road Station is an exception. It is bang in the centre of the industrial town, and folk from the country districts often make use of it for their Saturday shopping, thus avoiding the increasing annoyance of expensive parking. Nor do they have the problem of sitting in a stream of traffic at the end of a shopping spree which may coincide with traffic returning from football matches in Manchester. Our guide to the line was Harry Hatcher, the Chairman of the East Lancashire Railway Preservation Society. Harry explained that the Society provides the labour required to extend and maintain the line, whilst the East Lancashire Light Railway Company Limited actually operates the service. All assets are held by the East Lancashire Railway Trust, although he also pointed out that the line could not operate in its present form without the support and continued encouragement of the local councils.

Originally the line ran from Bury to Bacup via Ramsbottom and Rawtenstall, but was closed to passengers in July 1972, and to freight in 1980. By this time (fortunately) there was in existence an organisation which was able to rescue the railway.

In 1968 a Transport Museum had been set up based at Helmshore which, just like Topsy, grew and grew. In 1972 it was moved to Bury and housed opposite Bolton Street Station in a huge warehouse which had been constructed around 1840 and was thus almost a museum of the railway age in its own

Burnley Road, Bacup, around 1890.

right! It was intended to set out a clean and tidy display of old modes of transport with a collection of old steam locomotives, including one which was used by the Burnley Gasworks Company, plus an assortment of vintage buses, fire engines and cranes. The walls are covered with signs and signals, advertisements and artefacts, posters and points. And then the railway line closed. The idea of a living, breathing, mobile museum took root quickly, and the blessing and brass of the local council plus the free seat of willing skilled and unskilled workers soon meant that steam and old diesel locomotives were ready for the off. As usual in these cases keen railway folk purchased their own engines and brought them – often in bits – to the museum for restoration. Thus instead of a pristine shed we have a mucky, steamy, oil-smelling, noisy, busy, exciting, vibrant and irresistible hive of industry.

In July 1987 the dream came true as a steam train service along 4½ miles of track to Ramsbottom via Summerseat opened for business. In 1990 the line was extended to Rawtenstall but this will unfortunately, have to be the terminus of the line since the construction of a new complex of roads around the town has swallowed up the old track. This used to

The Quakers' Meeting House, Crawshawbooth.

travel along the Irwell Valley as far as Bacup. The present terminus, however, is so close to a supermarket that the line is bound to attract passengers, whilst tourists to the town will be able to enjoy the dry slopes of Ski-Rossendale and Helmshore Textile Museum.

Set in a pretty area of parkland, Ski-Rossendale commands a remarkable view over the Rossendale Valley. The centre is open all the year round and is frequented by beginners as well as experts keeping in shape before going out in search of continental snow. Expert tuition is always available and equipment can be hired. Advance booking is not required.

What a nostalgic feeling it must give to those who first started the Transport Museum at Helmshore to see the railway track reaching out from its new home in Bury back down the valley. Although the line has gone as far as possible in the Rawtenstall direction, there is some room for expansion from Rochdale to Heywood where there is an easy link into the BR network, and this will obviously open up the possibilities of running 'steam specials' which are becoming gradually more acceptable to B.R. For the present, however, we had to be

From the Peel Tower most of the Irwell Valley can be seen.

satisfied with a ride on the Red Rose Line between Ramsbottom and Bury.

Ramsbottom was provided with a brand-new station costing in excess of £100,000 and designed by Steven Lever, an architect with Bury Council. He went back to the original style of the East Lancashire Railway, and on its opening day (19th June 1989) it looked like a bit of Victorian England brought to life. Local firms were involved in the building of a complex which deserves to be a tourist attraction in its own right. There is a ticket office, waiting room, refreshingly clean toilets and a well-stocked souvenir and book shop.

Everyone concerned has done such a fine job that visitors, who are not aware of its recent construction, feel transported back to the early days of steam. 'There's nowt like these owld spots', we heard one old gentleman remark. 'They can't build these days like they could in th'owd days'.

'More often than not he would be right, but Ramsbottom's situation is a glorious exception to the rule. The staff of these restored railways have a real pride in their (unpaid) work and the ELR lads all sport a red rose in their lapels and ooze confidence and friendliness.

With a whistle and a wave of its guard's green flag the locomotive *Sir Robert Peel* built up steam and eased out of the station on the first lap of the 20-minute journey back to Bury. Passing sports fields and parks, the line heads out to Summerseat, surely one of the least spoiled villages in the country despite being so close to the A56. It is reached via the very narrow Bass Lane which has passing places along its steep length and is lined with splendid houses. In the dip a number of attractive cottages line the railway track and the derelict station shows how close this system came to oblivion. Tangles of rosebay willowherb, thistles, bramble and elder are everywhere.

Views from this section of the line show just how beautiful the valley of the Irwell is. Although it is still polluted along some of its course, there are beauty spots and many of these can be seen from the railway which crosses and recrosses the river several times. Typical of the beauty is the Waterside Hotel at Summerseat which overlooks the river; the restoration of this building has been very effectively done and is certain to make its contribution to the tourist potential of the area.

The leisurely pace of *Sir Robert Peel* allowed us the luxury of bird watching in comfort – in the green fields we saw a small flock of lapwings, a stately heron on the lookout for its lunch by the side of a small stream, and a kestrel hovering over the remains of an old lineside allotment. Around this we also saw a surprising number of rabbits. One of the real joys of travel on the steam railways must have been the sight of the flower displays on the stations – competitions were held amongst the staff to find the best of these and vegetable competitions were held too.

On the day of our visit, Bury's Bolton Street was as busy as on any day of its working life. Enthusiasts were working hard to restore the steam locomotive *Morning Star* and the stationary restaurant car and model railway shop were doing a roaring trade. Delightfully 1950s in their style, the bookshop and the booking office were also busy, and every noticeboard offered an interesting way of using the railway. Diesel weekends, Harry Hatcher told us, are proving increasingly popular, as are the Santa Specials which now require booking in advance. Schools are making more and more use of the line as a real working aid to projects on industrial archaeology, whilst those of us who are tired of the drudgery of modern-day industry join the reasonably priced Sunday Special with a meal at the Grants Arms in Ramsbottom.

Whenever we enjoy a quiet hour in the Grants Arms, we inevitably hear someone ask the question, 'Who was Grant?' Actually there were two Grants, and very fine adopted Lancashire Lads they were, to be sure. Never were two brothers more devoted than William and Charles Grant, who were immortalised by Charles Dickens as the Cheeryble brothers in *Nicholas Nickleby*. Born in Inverness of farming stock, but robbed of their inheritance by an horrendous flood, they journeyed south and found jobs in a print works (cloth printing) near Bury. Their ambition was to set up a business of their own, but the question was where? They decided upon Ramsbottom, some say by climbing a local hill and tossing a pointed stick in the air to see in which direction it fell. They went on to become millionaires. One reason for both their success and their popularity is that they never lost their common touch and were, as Dickens mentions, much loved by their workforce. Some historians are less impressed by the Grants and suggest that they sought fame and cared not for their workers.

Whenever we journey along the ELR, we wonder if the well-travelled Dickens ever watched the steam curling up from the chimneys of the engines into the smokey atmosphere which then hung over the Irwell Valley. Today the journey is dominated by the view of the Peel Monument which can be reached from either Ramsbottom or from Holcombe village. The best route to the tower is from Holcombe Moor car park on the right of the road between Holcombe Brook and Helmshore. Built in 1852 to commemorate the life of Sir Robert Peel (1788-1850), the tower stands 128 feet high. After a long period of neglect the tower has now been restored and is sometimes open to the public. What splendid views can be had from the stout structure, especially at weekends when the steam locomotives can be seen travelling along the valley bottom. Robert Peel was born in Bury and became one of the most influential Prime Ministers of the century. He repealed the Corn Laws and was also instrumental in setting up the police force, which became known as both Peelers and Bobbies!

Bury suffered more than most from the town planners of the 1960s and 1970s who seem to have been hellbent on making all our mill towns look alike. But there is still a grand old market where the best black puddings in the world, heavily dosed with vinegar and mustard, can be bought and eaten on the spot.

Bury made a healthy living but polluted the Irwell with its mills and factories turning out blankets, felt and high-quality notepaper. John Kay, the inventor of the flying shuttle, was born on the outskirts of Bury in 1704, and this ingenious device saved the operatives having to throw the shuttle from one side of the loom to the other.

We were as surprised as many to find in the late 1980s that Bury once had a substantial castle. It was situated just to the west of the Victorian parish church of St Mary the Virgin and at the rear of the White Lion Hotel. It is a great pity that the site was almost swamped by a drill hall constructed during the nineteenth century.

From Bury's point of view it is a pity that Henry VII defeated Richard III on the battlefield of Bosworth in 1485 because Thomas Pilkington backed the wrong side and his fortress was dismantled. There was a settlement hereabouts long before the Normans, there is a wealth of evidence, and many artefacts have been found and dated to the Bronze Age. A Roman road passes close by and heads off towards Darwen. The modern name, however, dates to the twelfth century when a Norman family named de Bury held the manor, and by 1360 the land was owned by the Pilkingtons, one of whom had married a Bury heiress.

It was the Peel family who first dragged Bury from being a green and fertile spot into becoming a dark place dominated by cotton. In 1770 Robert Peel set up the 'Ground Calico Printing Works', and Peel Yates and Tipping became so prosperous that their mills, print and bleach works dominated the whole of the Irwell Valley and provided the immense fortune on which Robert Peel was able to base his political career. Robert was born in 1788 and his substantial bronze statue dominates the Market Street area. Here also is a very good art gallery which was started by Thomas Wrigley, a prominent paper manufacturer, in the nineteenth century; he was also a vigorous supporter of compulsory education for all. The attractive Town Hall is modern and was opened by the Queen in 1954.

Although he invented the flying shuttle, John Kay had no business head and he died almost penniless in France, his grave unmarked. Fortunately his native town has not forgotten him and a bronze memorial graces the delightful Kay Gardens which bloom like an oasis in the centre of what was an industrial complex and follow the river all the way into Manchester.

CHAPTER 6

Around Bolton

Our interest in Bolton began in the early 1960s following an appointment to teach biology at Smithills Grammar School, recently constructed as one of three schools in old grounds of the historic Smithills Hall, the pupils occasionally attending morning assembly in the chapel of the medieval building.

Surrounded by a wooded nature trail, Smithills Hall is built on an easily defended hill above Ravenden Clough. The earliest building was the work of the Knights Hospitallers, but the present hall dates from the fourteenth century. There have been alterations since, but the medieval hall really is magnificent its quatrefoil decoration dating from around 1350. Many of the rooms have beautifully preserved sixteenth-century carvings. The chapel attached to the house was burned down but was rebuilt in 1856. In 1938 Smithills was bought by Bolton Corporation and has served as a museum ever since. The old stables and coach houses have been converted into an attractive restaurant reached through an archway and overlooking a courtyard on which stand accurately restored and brightly painted stagecoaches.

One sad event in the annals of the Hall which at one time was called Smithells was the death of the martyr George Marsh. In the bigoted times of Tudor England it was usually the Catholics who suffered, but Marsh was a Protestant who perished in the repressive times of Bloody Mary. Whilst under investigation at Smithills he refused to repent and is said to have firmly stamped his foot to emphasise a point, making an impression on the stone floor. This 'bloody footprint' became even more obvious after his execution and it can still be seen near the door of the dining room.

Bolton has a second half-timbered building which attracts large numbers of visitors. Hall-i'-the'-wood is reached along a well signposted road lined with modern houses. Despite the urban sprawl around it, Hall-i'-th'-wood is surrounded by its own garden and still retains a sylvan atmosphere. In this late fifteenth-century house lived Samuel Crompton (1753-1827), one of several tenants, and who invented the spinning mule in 1799. This could produce yarn which was both strong and fine enough to produce muslin and which gave Lancashire's cotton industry an unassailable advantage over its competitors. At first the machine was called the muslin wheel. Its efficiency was never in doubt, but the local handloom weavers saw it as a threat, and gave Samuel many a fright as they plotted to smash his machine. Such a building ought to be preserved both in its own right and because of its illustrious occupant.

In 1899 Lord Leverhulme bought the house and paid for its preservation before giving it to Bolton as a museum. It now houses a fine collection of Crompton's and other textile inventions but the Tudor woodwork is in prime condition also and the collection of eighteenth-century furniture is fascinating. There is a cheese press and a set of cheese trays on castors, a large mangle and an ingenious box chair which also served as a bacon cupboard. Samuel's talents were not entirely directed at work, for also on display in the hall is an organ which he built entirely by himself. No wonder that as he often worked late into the night, the locals were convinced that there was a wizard at work. Crompton was born to a poor family in a cottage still standing at Firwood Fold off Crompton Way, and he was such a poor businessman that he also died without a penny to his name whilst others used his invention to amass large fortunes.

The town of Bolton itself has a long and impressive history antedating the rise of King Cotton. Bolton-Le-Moors, as it was once called was first settled during the Bronze Age and was a moderately-sized market town at the time of the Civil War when one of the bloodiest episodes of the troubles occurred. The Royalists, under the command of James Stanley, the Earl of Derby, took the town and many of the parliamentary supporters were massacred. When the King's men were defeated, Derby was brought back to Bolton and there he was executed, his severed head and body being returned in separate caskets to the family church at Ormskirk where they were interred. Whilst waiting for his punishment on 15th October 1651, Derby was kept at Ye Olde Man and Scythe Inn on Churchgate which dates back to 1251 and still stands today,

Jumbles Reservoir was opened in 1971 to provide water for industry and is also used by anglers and boaters.

although a great deal of rebuilding has gone on since. Parts of it, however, are obviously medieval.

But Bolton, just like other Lancashire towns, was an eventual product of the cotton boom. Its main efforts were concentrated on the spinning of high-quality cotton, leaving Oldham to specialise in the equally necessary coarser yarns. Once more we see money poured into civic buildings, the Town Hall being designed by William Hill in the usual classical style and opened in 1873. Most of Lancashire during this period must have been a gigantic building site with the wealth from cotton literally spinning off jobs to quarrymen and construction workers.

Some light can be thrown on what the early development of Bolton must have been like by visiting the village of Barrow Bridge situated just off the Bolton ring road. It was once called Dean Mills and was set on the network of packhorse routes which traversed the area. There were coalmines and quarries hereabouts, and in the late eighteenth century a farmer named Robert Eatock cut sixty-three steps down to the Dean Brook which was the boundary between Halliwell and Horwich, the latter having its period of glory later, in the days when steam

Rivington Hall and Park attract thousands of weekend visitors.

locomotives were built there. These steps originally served to carry stone and fuel down to the developing mills which took over from the weavers' cottages. In the 1850s Gardener and Bazley built Dean Mills and employed more than 1,000 people for whom a purpose-built village was provided. This inspired Disraeli's novel *Coningsby*, and we feel it may also have given William Hesketh Lever (1851-1925) the idea for Port Sunlight.

William was born at No 16 Wood Street, Bolton on 19th September 1851, the son of a grocer with a strict Nonconformist faith and a typical Victorian belief that a son should follow in his father's footsteps. William was 33 before he managed to loose the family ties and ask his father to lend him the money to specialise in one aspect of the grocery business – soap. In retrospect we can see why the father, with a business to run and seven daughters to support, was reluctant to lay out good money on a scheme to produce soap, especially as his son was insisting on a new method of production. Instead of using the traditional animal fat as the base for his soap, the young fool was proposing to use vegetable oil from coconuts! There must have been some softness in the father because he finally agreed to provide £4000, not enough to buy a factory but enough to rent premises in Wigan and produce what William

Turton Tower – One of Lancashire's most historic houses, now open as a museum.

called Sunlight Soap. Where William Hesketh Lever beat all competitors was in his realisation of the need for advertising. Having a good product was one thing, but this was nothing if nobody knew about it. It worked, and inside four years his premises were not large enough to meet demand but the substantial profits enabled him to buy land on the Wirral bank of the Mersey, and what became Unilever and Port Sunlight village was begun. He successfully defended his product in the courts as jealous competitors copied his unique wrapper, and to cut out the middleman's profit he purchased 200,000 acres of land in the Solomon Islands and more than 1,750,000 acres in the Congo where the nuts required to produce the oil for his soap were grown.

During the First World War the market for margarine, which was a German invention, was cut off and Lever was asked to produce a British equivalent. Never one to do things by half, he bought a whaling company to ensure his supply of raw material, and whilst he was about it he set up a fishing business as a sideline which eventually became Mac Fisheries.

The humbly born son of a Bolton grocer was elevated to the peerage as Lord Leverhulme, and apart from being a model for hard work he left more permanent records of his industry

The well house is the only one of Hollinshead Hall's buildings which still stands.

in the form of Port Sunlight as well as Rivington, now a Country Park on the outskirts of Horwich, and overlooked by the famous Pike. The 1,190-foot (363m) summit has been a beacon point for centuries and was in readiness at the time of the Armada in 1588. Actually there seem to be two towers here, but the lower building is a pigeon tower, once part of Leverhulme's gardens, whilst the Pike itself is reached along a well trodden and gently sloping footpath. The communications masts on nearby Winter Hill are also prominent. There are a number of excellent car parks.

Each Good Friday, crowds of people make the pilgrimmage to enjoy Pike Fair, an informal and highly colourful gathering. Below can be seen an ingenious complex of eight reservoirs which each day since the nineteenth century have provided 11.5 million gallons per day to the Liverpool area.

Part of the old village is now under Rivington reservoir, but several historic buildings remain in the valley which has been settled since the Bronze Age. Rivington Hall Barn and Great House Barn are two of Britain's few remaining Saxon cruck-barns which are supported by huge boughs of oak. Great House Barn is now a visitor centre with a cafe. The church also has Saxon origins although it was rebuilt in 1541 and altered

Smithills Hall about 1940.

again in 1884, when part of the old village green was swallowed up by the new vicarage. The stocks now stand on what remains of the green. Rivington Hall was rebuilt in 1774 and is now a restaurant, but the adjacent old barn was retained.

In 1899 some 364 acres of Rivington estate were bought by Lord Leverhulme, and by 1901 he had built a wooden bungalow on the slopes of the Pike. In July 1913 whilst the Levers were dining with King George V at the home of Lord Derby, a suffragette named Edith Rigby set fire to the bungalow, which was known to the locals as Roynton Cottage. Within a year a more substantial structure was built mainly of stone, containing a minstrel's gallery, a circular ballroom and a flat concrete roof. The house was often thrown open to the public, and this and the oriental-style gardens were a source of joy to locals and the Levers alike. The pigeon tower already referred to dominated the gardens; it was built in 1910 and the whole ambitious enterprise was completed by 1922. What would have happened if Lord Lever had not died in 1925 or left behind an heir we cannot tell, but what is certain is that the house and gardens fell into disrepair. In 1947 they were bought by Liverpool Corporation who promptly demolished the house. In the recent past North West Water have encouraged volunteers to work on the gardens, and something of the old splendour and a great deal of the atmosphere are being regenerated.

Lever did, however, leave the park itself to the people of Bolton and also commemorated his Merseyside connections by building a full-size replica of the long-demolished Liverpool Castle overlooking Rivington reservoir. He also built the 'folly' or Pike on top of the hill which dominates the area for miles around.

Turton Tower is neither a replica nor a folly and is another fine example of a half-timbered house. It is situated near Bromley Cross within easy reach of Bolton, although it is actually part of the Blackburn museum service. It is open to the public, and there is plenty of car parking.

Overlooking a drive bordered by beech and horse chestnut, Turton Tower is a Tudor house built around an early fifteenth-century pele tower, designed as defence against the Scots. Some additions were made by the Orrel family and by Humphrey Chetham (1580-1653), the Manchester textile merchant and moneylender who bought Turton but allowed the Orrels to remain in residence. Used as a farmhouse during the eighteenth century, Turton was eventually bought and restored by the industrialist, James Kay. When the Bolton to Blackburn railway was built in the 1840s, Kay insisted that the bridges close to the tower be suitably castellated to remain in keeping with the house. In 1903 Sir Lees Knowles bought Turton and it was given by his widow to the local district council in 1930. This was absorbed in 1974 by Blackburn Council who now run it as a museum. There are fine collections of armour, splendid Tudor and Victorian furniture and a remarkable German chandelier made from fallow deer antlers. The dining room often rings with the laughter of schoolchildren dressed as Tudor or Victorian gentlefolk. What a lovely way to learn history!

Nearby is Pickup Bank, a tiny hamlet perched on a breezy hillside dotted with sheep farms and tastefully restored cottages. Old Rosin's Inn, an imposing and isolated building, once a farm house, overlooks a fertile valley lined with trees which screen disused mills and their water-filled lodges, now the home of wintering wildfowl with breeding coot and great crested grebe. From around 1830 the Inn was called The Duke

This is the Touches Stone dating from the 9th century and from which Tockholes takes its name.

of Wellington, but at the beginning of this century the landlord had a band and used resin to polish the instruments and the dance floor. Locals enjoyed visiting 'Old Rosin's', and this interesting dialect name was eventually adopted.

Tockholes is also an interesting village between Bolton and Blackburn. Close to the Victoria Inn, School Lane descends steeply to Ivy Cottages, draped by sweet-smelling rambling roses. Next to the cottages is the United Reformed Chapel founded in 1662 but rebuilt in 1710 and again in 1880. Here was an isolated centre of Nonconformity in times of great intolerance. The parish church with its unique lance-shaped windows is reached along a narrow lane beyond the chapel. The church was rebuilt in 1832, and an unusual feature is an outdoor pulpit, a relic of the days when large summer congregations could not be accommodated inside. Buried close to the pulpit is John Osbaldeston who invented the weft fork, a device enabling the powered cotton loom to weave fancy shapes. Tockholes has many old handloomers' cottages which have been individually restored, their woodwork brightly painted and their gardens stocked with scented smock, wallflowers, sweet peas and hollyhocks.

Just beyond Tockholes is Roddlesworth Nature Trail with a large car park, information centre and picnic site near the Royal Arms Inn and bus stop. A path which was once the old coach drive winds through shaded woodland to open spaces where curlew, cuckoo, merlin and meadow pipit have all been sighted by birdwatchers. A trail leaflet can be purchased from the Royal Arms or the information centre which indicates the cobbled coach road and the ruins of the once-magnificent eighteenth-century Hollinshead Hall.

During late 1990s and early 1991 the ruins of the Hall and its associated farm were excavated and tidied up, whilst the so-called wishing well has happily survived the ravages of time. This resembles a small Georgian chapel built into a hillside which to the casual observer seems to be in danger of damage from flood water. Actually the building was constructed around a medieval well whose waters were thought to be a cure for eye complaints and which attracted pilgrims from miles around.

It is hard to explore this area without becoming obsessed by water, and there are now marked trails around all the local reservoirs, none more impressive than the most recent construction at Jumbles just off the A676 Bradshaw Road as it descends towards Bolton. There is ample car parking, toilets and a visitor centre. Jumbles reservoir was opened only in 1971 and swamped the large Horrobin mill complex and bleach works which must have badly polluted Bradshaw Brook whose waters were dammed to produce the reservoir. Jumbles is a triumph for the multiple use of water. It provides 10 million gallons of compensation water for industry and is not used for drinking, thus enabling angling, boating and other water-based activities to be encouraged; a shallow area is also set out for wildlife. Gone is all the dirt and grime of industry, and what were once almost derelict workers' houses are now much sought-after cottages set into a landscape which, although modern, already has an ancient feel about it. Things cannot have been so peaceful here since the days of the farmer who did a little handloom weaving on the side. There are many footpaths plus a bridleway leading out from a riding centre and stables on the banks of the reservoir. Further improvements are in hand at Jumbles to provide a larger information centre, a book shop and a cafe. Lancashire's countryside will again demonstrate its now irresistible resilience.

CHAPTER 7

Around Wigan

Until very recently the mention of Wigan produced a mixture of mirth and insult, but also with just a pinch of grudging admiration. The first two concern the Pier and the last the greatest Rugby League team in the world.

George Formby senior is said to have been the first to refer to Wigan Pier and by all accounts he did not mean to insult his home town but merely sought to make the amusing and tongue-in-cheek point that it compared favourably with Blackpool where most local folk spent their holidays which were known locally as the Wakes Week. When George Orwell wrote *The Road to Wigan Pier* in 1937, it was meant as a political statement and depicted the town in a none too flattering light. We wonder what he would feel if he returned to the Pier complex now as it basks in the deserved glory of being the most attractive visitor centre along the whole length of the Leeds to Liverpool Canal. What would he think of the pub named after him which is such a popular part of the set-up? In the days when Wigan was one of the busiest coalmining areas in the country and also manufactured textiles, most people came home black and no washing line was safe from sooty fall-out.

If Wiganers worked hard, they certainly played hard. It was said that if you went to a pit shaft and whistled, the first thirteen lads to reach the surface would take only ten minutes to blend into a rough, tough, Rugby League team.

The rest of the professional rugby game looks to Wigan as the pinacle of the profession. Our fathers told us of the great Jim Sullivan, a full-back with a kick like a mule and a tackle like a sledgehammer. We ourselves remember the elegant skills of Eric Ashton, and the flying bulk of winger Billy Boston. The Central Park ground has its present-day heroes, none more exciting than Ellery Hanley, not the heaviest loose forward we have ever seen but around 14 stone of twisting sinew and surprising pace. Not for nothing has he been described as the most complete player in the world.

Haigh Hall – A taste of elegant Wigan.

Despite its rapid development during the Industrial Revolution, Wigan is one of the oldest towns in Lancashire, and some of its history and that of its surrounding villages is still evident and can be found by those with the energy to spend time in the search. Much of its urban beauty – and there is plenty – has been restored by the efforts of the Wigan Groundwork Trust, which was formed in 1984.

The early history of Wigan takes us back to prehistoric times when most of what is now Lancashire was hillsides clothed in trees with the river valleys a combination of unhealthy marshland and water. The Celtic Brigantes were here until the first century AD and had a settlement on the site of modern Wigan which was taken over by the Romans who built a small town called Coccium. Hard proof of this settlement has been rather slow in coming but recent excavations in the area around Millgate have revealed a short section of road, and the remains of metal smelting furnaces have also been found.

In 1848, during the construction of a gasworks, burial urns were unearthed, and an altar used in the worship of Mithras has been found incorporated into the parish church.

After the departure of the Roman legions the town seems to have been part of Anglo-Saxon England fluctuating between

Mercia and Northumbria which in those far-off and troubled times seemed constantly to be squabbling with each other. The precise origin of the new name Wigan does seem a little obscure, but most scholars accept that it derives from a personal name, perhaps Wic-Ham, either Anglo-Saxon or perhaps of Breton origin. A number of natives from the latter region settled in these parts during and just after the Conquest.

Wigan was granted a market charter by Henry III in 1246. By 1295 the town had two MPs, although the Rector of All Saints parish church, who was actually the Bishop of Chester, held the reins of power locally, and it was only in 1860 that the town felt confident enough to govern itself totally.

As befitting a town of substance, Wigan played its part, often controversially, in the political and religious events of the day. At the Reformation, for example, Wigan and the surrounding manors remained solidly Catholic, and whilst they were not officially supported by the Bishop of Chester, there was a lack of criticism which is perhaps just as significant. The education hereabouts was also solid, and the traditions of Wigan Grammar School were established in 1597.

During the Civil War, Wigan was firmly behind Charles I, although it did object to the King forcing it to pay Ship Money, which to an inland town did not seem quite fair. It also thought that one man one vote was more in keeping with the times than the divine right of kings which was the Stuart philosophy. The King, however had Catholic connections and this was a factor when it came to taking sides in the conflict between the monarch and the Protestant parliament.

The leader of the Royalist movement in the Wigan area had no rival: the Earl of Derby, with his home at Lathom House on the outskirts of the town, was a favourite of the King. Wigan was obviously his base, and from there he could plan his infamous attack on Bolton which was just as staunch in its support for Parliament. The tragic events which took place there have been described in Chapter 6.

Wigan, on the other hand, fared badly at the hands of the Roundheads. In 1643 it was entered by parliamentary troops, its moot hall and church were looted, and its then substantial fortifications were reduced to rubble and were never restored. It was probably this destruction which made Lord Derby deal

Mab's Cross – A reminder of Medieval Wigan.

so harshly with Bolton in the following year, which in turn cost him his life. Although Wigan had lost its fortifications, its strategic importance remained, since it straddled the vital north-south route which followed the line of the present A49.

One claim to fame which Wigan has is not so well documented or remembered as it ought to be. It was here on 25th August 1651 that the last battle of the Civil War in Lancashire was fought. The Battle of Wigan Lane is commemorated by a monument which stands on the spot where Sir Thomas Tyldesley, a respected officer in the army of the Earl of Derby, was killed by the forces led by the Parliamentarian Colonel Robert Lilburne.

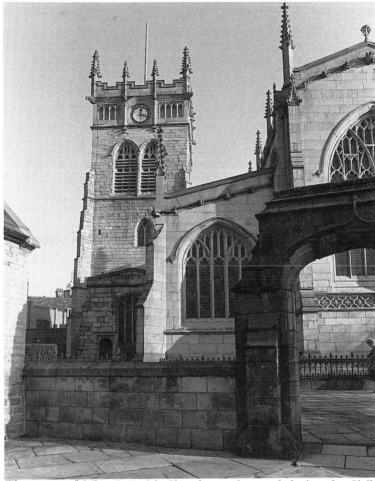

The tower of Wigan's Parish Church was damaged during the Civil War.

Another monument of interest situated on Standishgate is Mab's Cross, a slab of stone with a fascinating and tragic story to tell. The River Douglas meanders close to Haigh Hall just outside Wigan. 'Haigh' was a Saxon word meaning an enclosure, and even today it is surrounded by attractive and mainly broadleaved woodlands. In 1188 Haigh was owned by Hugh Le Norreys, but it was Mabel, the daughter of his grandson, who brought fame and perhaps a certain amount of

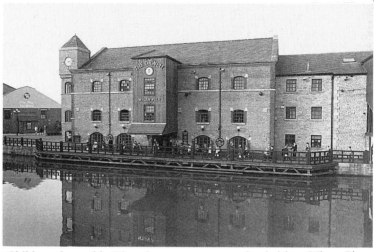

Children dressed in Victorian costume on a school visit to Wigan Pier.

fable to the family. In 1295 she married into the Anglo-Saxon family of de Bradshaigh. Her husband Sir William went away – some say to a crusade, others that he was banished – and was absent from 1315 to 1322. As he was missing, presumed dead, Mab remarried a man described as a Welsh knight, although in those days Welsh referred not to a nationality but meant a stranger or a newcomer. Sir William returned and, according to legend, pursued the knight and killed him at a spot called the 'bloody stone' at Newton-le-Willows. The facts, however, suggest that Sir William, never a peaceful soul, was himself killed on this spot in 1333. Whatever the truth of the matter, Mab was ordered by her confessor to walk barefoot once a week to the cross in Standishgate. The lady was still alive in 1348 and the cross was being referred to as Mab's Cross in a deed of 1403 when the Haigh estate was owned by her nephew. Her tomb and that of her legal husband are in Wigan parish church.

At the time of the Battle of Wigan Lane the Bradshaighs were still in residence, and when Charles II was restored to the throne he did not forget either Wigan or Sir Roger Bradshaigh – a new borough charter was given and the knight appointed as Mayor.

Apart from his bravery in the great battle, Roger's energies

The water-bus from Wigan Pier turns under the bridge below Trencherfield Mill.

were also directed into the construction of what became known as the Great Sough. This came about because of the need to extract the increasingly valuable coal on his estate without causing flooding of neighbouring lands, and the project which began very tentatively in 1652 was finished in 1670 amid much well-deserved backslapping and hailed as one of the finest scientific enterprises of its age.

The usual and very unsightly method of mining had been to dig surface channels, but Sir Roger constructed an underground tunnel around two-thirds of a mile long, 6 feet wide and 4 feet high (1.05km by 1.8 metres by 1.2 metres), draining the mines into the Yellow Brook just before its confluence with the River Douglas, itself a tributary of the Ribble. The channel was regularly inspected until 1923 when water levels reached the roof, but it still fulfils its original function and drains the old workings which have long since closed.

Haighs was no ordinary coal but of a type called cannel, very rich in volatile substances which meant that it burned almost without smoke. It did, however, have another property which made it even more valuable. When first mined, it is quite dull, but cannel is surprisingly clean to the touch and is capable of taking a very high gloss. It will also cut easily and therefore has

Pennington Flash at Leigh is a haven for wildlife, set among a background of coal mines.

been used to fashion lovely ornaments. We have had a go at this and have found it delightful to work with, which makes us wonder why Wigan cannel has not proved to have as much sales potential as the pieces cut from the Blue John mines in Derbyshire or from Whitby jet.

When the last Sir Roger Bradshaig died in 1770, the estate passed into the hands of 10-year-old Elizabeth Dalrymple who, when she was 20, married Alexander Lindsay, the 23rd Earl of Crawford, who managed Haigh very well, even setting up a foundry fired by his own coal. Wigan had a proud history of metal working and was famous for its pewterware as well as for the manufacture of bells carried by the lead animals on the packhorse trails. Later on many 'milestones' were made from cast iron, and many of these have recently been restored and painted white, standing on the roads into the town as a proud link with its past.

Haigh Foundry also did the castings for the famous Laxey Wheel in the Isle of Man, now a tourist attraction, but its original purpose was to pump water from the lead mines which were up to 1800 feet (548 metres) deep. Work was also done for the first Mersey Tunnel.

James, the 24th Earl of Crowford, became Baron Wigan of

A 'Milestone' forged at the Haigh foundry.

Haigh Hall, and it was he who replaced the historic half-timbered hall with the present house between 1830 and 1849. In 1947 the house and grounds were bought by Wigan Corporation, and it is now one of the finest Country Parks to be found anywhere in England. In the 250 acres there are secluded woodland walks where time appears to have stood still, but there are also modern facilities including picnic sites, a miniature zoo, a butterfly house and an 18-hole golf course which has proved more than a match for us, but our friends would not be surprised at that. Haigh Hall will also cater for weddings and other functions, and it is hard to find anywhere more attractive for a once-in-a-lifetime event.

Wigan also has another fine Country Park at Pennington Flash near the mining town of Leigh whose origins are in complete contrast to Haigh. We enjoyed making television films about it during the mid-1980s and found the ex-miner Eric Staniforth to be a warden with humour and enough local knowledge to talk to the tough youngsters in their own language and thus ensure that they respected what was being done for the local environment.

Pennington Flash is an area of 170 acres of water one mile to the south-west of Leigh, and since 1981 it has been incorporated into a Country Park of over 1,000 acres. At one time the area was entirely devoted to agriculture, the low-lying fields being divided by the meanderings of Hey Brook. Once the Leeds to Liverpool Canal had been constructed towards the end of the eighteenth century, a branch was cut to Leigh; this now constitutes the northern extremity of the park and overlooks Bickershaw Colliery which was one of the reasons for the canal branch being cut.

Extensive mining, particularly prior to nationalisation, led to subsidence and flooding. Wildfowl and other marsh birds are never slow to take advantage of such an ideal habitat, but their populations were initially kept at low levels by the uncontrolled activities of local shooters. Thanks to firm but understanding wardening, shooting has been very much reduced and wildfowl numbers are increasing. Ambitious but successful landscaping of old spoil heaps and associated colliery railway tracks has produced a variety of other habitats, especially indigenous hardwoods, but there are also some stands of conifers. As they mature, such areas are bound to increase the variety of species found around the edge of the water.

On the Flash itself anglers and boating interests have both been catered for, but areas of shallow water and reed beds have been reserved for the birds and are carefully protected. Encouraged by the chance of a good day's birdwatching from well-sited hides, increasing numbers of ornithologists are visiting the Flash, and little now escapes their sharp eyes. The Dalmatian pelican spotted in August 1970 was not accepted as a new British record as it was doubtless an escapee from a collection.

There is an Information Centre with exhibits and providing details of the footpaths which run through the park and affording views over stretches of water including the well-named Grebe Lodge which is a popular haven for both little and great crested grebe, especially when sailing is taking place on the open stretches. Some 10 to 12 pairs breed at Pennington, and the winter population is much higher but often declines dramatically during adverse winters. J.D. Wilson pointed out to us that local dabchicks have developed nocturnal habits by moving down Pennington Brook which is illuminated by adjacent street lights. There are usually between 5 and 8 pairs of great crested grebes plus around 25 non-breeding individuals which summer on the Flash. In the autumn they are joined by birds from other areas, numbers usually peaking during October with the 87 recorded on 12 October 1980 being the county record for Lancashire. After this initial concentration numbers decline as the winter progresses, which suggests that Pennington may be a post-breeding collecting point from which birds spread out to other stretches of water in the surrounding district including Scotsman's Flash, Wigan and Lightshaw Flash, Leigh. A low ebb of between 15 and 20 birds is reached in the depths of winter but rises again to around 40 between March and May. There have also been summer sightings of black-necked grebes, which has led to speculation about breeding.

Perhaps the most worrying feature of the present-day Flash is the failure of the mute swan to breed successfully. It really ought to be a regular breeder but the fact that it is not is due to the attentions of vandals and perhaps the sheer presence – albeit innocent – of anglers. The effect of lead shot cannot be discounted, although now that this has been made illegal, swan populations are bound to increase.

The main entrance to the Flash, which has a spacious car park overlooking the water, is off the A572 St Helens road in the vicinity of its junction with the recently constructed Leigh By-Pass. The Leeds to Liverpool Canal also now serves as a green corridor running through the town and bringing wildlife into the centre. There has also been a great deal of restoration work on canalside villages, especially Crook, Gathurst and Appley Bridge. Disused railway lines have also been reclaimed as linear nature reserves, one of the finest being the Leigh to

Standish Church.

Tyldesley and the strangely named Whelley Loop Line. These areas are also now catering for cyclists and horse riders as well as walkers.

Thus Wigan and district seems to have come almost full circle from countryside, through the black days of the Industrial Revolution to emerge during the last twenty years to take its place on the fringes of the green revolution.

By far the best place to discover Wigan's industrial history is Wigan Pier. There is so much to be seen and although its origins may have been lost in the smog of industry, there is no doubting its present or indeed its future importance to the economy and pride of Wigan. The mill at the Pier houses concerts, festivals and conferences. Behind the complex is Trencherfield Mill, still fired almost daily by the world's largest steam mill engine still working. And there is 'The Way We Were' exhibition, opened by the Queen in 1986. This is a museum with a difference, full of hustle, bustle and fact, historical squalor, science and fun. Teams of resident professional actors take the part of schoolmistress – we got on the wrong side of one dragon – colliers and their wives, devotees of the co-operative movement and cotton operatives. To do it justice, one visit to Wigan Pier is not enough, and it would need a full volume to itself. One thing is for sure – Orwell's road to Wigan Pier has long gone. Even the roads out of Wigan lead these days, not to grimy suburbs but to attractive places including Ashton-in-Makerfield, Aspull, Astley, Hindley and Pemberton, and not least among these is historic Standish.

The shape of this old market town can be seen by standing at the ancient cross, in front of which are the stocks and a plaque marking the position of the old well. To one side of the cross is Worthington's butcher's shop neatly whitewashed and now selling superb Lancashire cheese. This was built in 1703 as a thatched hotel, called the Eagle and Child, but has been used as a butcher's since it lost its licence in 1916. The Black Bull Hotel is still open for business as is the Lychgate Tavern situated behind the cross with the impressive parish church to the left. What a fine old building this is, entered via the Peace Gate, put up by public subscription and now commemorating the dead of two world wars, but built of red sandstone in 1926.

Above the entrance to the church itself is a sundial bearing the inscription 'Let no passing cloud of bitterness, Thine accostom'd serenity o'vershadow'. Beneath this is a Bible carved in stone. The church is dedicated to St Wilfrid and its scale and style indicate its once vital importance to the area. The first mention of a church on this site is in 1205, although it was rebuilt between 1582 and 1589. The steeple is an example of Victorian flamboyance.

It is the interior, however, which reflects the history of the area, as it is richly furnished with the trappings of influential local families including Wrightingtons, Chisnalls, Shevingtons and, of course, the Standish's themselves. There is the fine tomb of Edward Wrightington whose estate is now the base of the famous hospital specialising in hip replacements.

Set into a wall is a stone plaque commemorating another family which when translated from the Latin reads:

Edward Chisnall of Chisnall Square,
A very distinguished man,
A leader under the auspices of Charles
King and Martyr, A brave defender
Of the Manarchy and a learned
apologist of religion.

In the siege of Lathom
He bravely snatched from the enemy
A fire-breathing monster.
In the Catholic history which he wrote
He even now defends the Anglican church
as truly catholic.

He died on the 3rd March of our Redemption
1653 in the year of his age 35.
Mindful of such bravery and piety
his eldest son,
Edward Chisnall
of Chisnall, soldier, erected this marble.

Obviously the words of a brave young man in the anti-Royalist days of the Commonwealth, but if the Chisnalls helped shape the old county, then the Standish family surely helped to shape the history of the New World. The latter came to the area with the blessing of William of Normandy with whom they crossed the Channel, and Ralph de Standish was knighted in the fourteenth century for his part in putting down the Peasants' Revolt and became warden of Scarborough Castle. There was a Standish at Agincourt in 1415, but the family's most famous son was a vital member of the Pilgrim Fathers who sailed them on the *Mayflower* in 1620. Miles Standish had proved to be a bonny fighter and was employed to defend the Brethren against hostile Indians. The Americans still honour his memory.

In view of the family's strong Catholic faith, it seems strange

The Chisnall Memorial, Standish Church.

to find Miles defending Protestants, but we suppose that Christians must have decided to band together to fight the heathen. The home-based family, however, entered into no such truce and were heavily implicated in events leading up to the 1715 Jacobite rebellion, Standish Hall had its own priests, and illegal masses were regularly held. There is an old house near the village which has three black cats painted on the gable.

end. These date back to the time when an ornamental cat was placed in the window whenever a mass was being celebrated in the hall. This was standard practice throughout the country, and this is probably the origin of the Red Cat Inn on the road between Chorley and Blackburn.

In 1920 the last Standish died without heir and the Hall was put up for sale. Alas, it failed to meet the asking price and the Tudor section was demolished along with the chapel and transported to America. To find the most impressive Standish memorial we would need to journey to Duxbury in America. Here is the grave of Miles Standish who died in his bed at a ripe old age but his tomb befits a soldier and is surrounded by four ancient cannons and a supply of ammunition. There is also a tower dedicated to him in Duxbury but English historians seem in doubt whether his origins were at Duxbury Hall, now beneath a golf course near Chorley, or at Standish itself. Can we sit on the fence and suggest that Miles would know both – after all they are situated quite close together.

Close to Standish are the Worthington Lakes, likely to be one of Lancashire's most important projects for the 1990s. These are disused reservoirs which once served bleach mills, but they are now an angler's paradise soon also to have an information centre and a network of walks ideal for birdwatchers.

The industrial history of Wigan may be black, its Rugby team cherry and white, but its future is bright, green and rosy.

CHAPTER 8

Around Blackburn

Working for a provincial newspaper has many advantages for anyone wishing to extend a countryscene column into a portrait of the area. There is the chance to talk to people who remember the old days and to local historians who piece together the period long before the industry came for instance, to the valley of the Blackwater (the Black burn) and polluted this little tributary of the River Darwen, itself a tributory of the Ribble.

At the time we were preparing this book we were also making a television film about the Ribble and the *Lancashire Evening Telegraph* was earning a national award for its efforts in setting up a Grimewatch campaign in association with Crown-Berger paints and the Keep Britain Tidy Group. Being judges helped us to see what splendid efforts are being made by East Lancashire individuals and authorities in following the example of Wigan in making use of the canal corridor and reclaiming derelict sites to bring the countryside back into the town.

The area around Eanam Wharf has been transformed and it is possible to enjoy a bar snack and a drink in a concourse, once a warehouse, overlooking the canal. Nearby the dray horses owned by Thwaites Brewery are stabled and there is nothing we like better than to spend a morning with the horses and their blacksmith, especially on the days when they are preparing to visit a show, but no one should ever forget that they are working horses which actually deliver beer.

Opposite the stable is the Packet House, a hostelry which played an important role in the days when the Leeds to Liverpool Canal was the vital commercial artery of the town.

In its prime Blackburn was the biggest weaving town in the world, many 'ordinary' lads made very fast fortunes, and of these none had more character than Billy Grimshaw who, when he equipped his mills with new looms, had the old ones taken out into the yard and smashed into scrap. This was to prevent foreign competitors, particularly from Japan and India, from

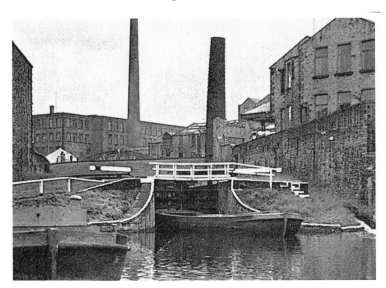

Above: Blackburn is now restoring its stretch of the Leeds to Liverpool Canal, but it is too late to save the open-air market and the new complex looks like that of the most other towns. Gone are the tripe shops which we loved to frequent.

using cheap machines and labour to undercut his prices. Among the visitors from India who came to Lancashire to study textile manufacture was one named Mahatma Gandhi who toured Blackburn and Darwen between 21st and 23rd September 1931. Considering how the Lancashire cotton industry has declined, perhaps we should try to reincarnate Billy Grimshaw!

Blackburn's place in textile history was due in no small measure to John James Hargreaves, born near Blackburn in 1745, who began life as a weaver but showed great ability as a carpenter. Although Hargreaves died poor, the cotton industry was much enriched by his life's work. At first textile spinning was not nearly so efficient as weaving, which had literally been revolutionised by Kay's invention of the flying shuttle. The thread to feed the looms, however, was still spun one thread at a time on a spinning wheel operated by girls and women, from which process we get the name of 'spinster'.

Whether there is any truth in the story or not, there is the lovely tale of how in 1764 James Hargreaves was watching his little daughter Jenny when she slipped and knocked over her mother's spinning wheel. He noticed that the wheel kept on revolving even when the spindle was in an upright position. Then came the flash of inspiration which separates a genius from the rest of us mortals. If the wheel drove one spindle in the upright position, then why not several? Being a carpenter, he soon produced a working spinning Jenny, and never again would the weaver have to wait for the spinster. But this did not make him popular, those whose work was made easier still saw it as a threat to their livelihood, and James had to flee to Nottingham where he patented his device, but not before others had copied it. Hargreaves, the father of the cotton spinning boom, therefore gained much fame but no fortune at all.

Anyone who wants to see examples of early machines should visit the Lewis Textile Museum in the centre of Blackburn. Here can be seen a spinning Jenny and also a carding machine, invented by Hargreaves in 1760. Carding is a method by which the tangled fibres are combed straight so that they can be easily spun.

Blackburn has lost most of its cotton-spinning industry, its

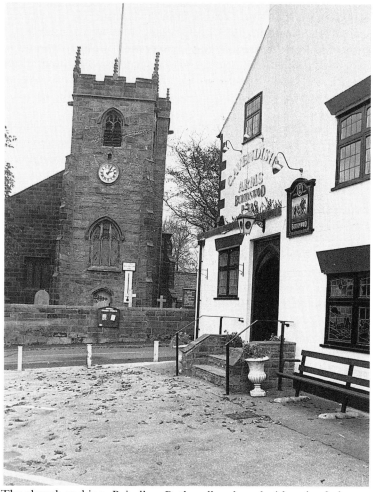

The church and inn, Brindle – Both well endowed with stained glass.

population has declined, and its football team is no longer the wonder of its age. None of the mill towns has, however, lost its pride. The Workers' Educational Associations still hold classes in industrial archaeology and natural history, and light engineering industries provide a reasonable number of jobs in a difficult employment situation throughout Europe.

One thing which Blackburn lacks is a manor house of

significance, only Witton, now a Country Park, offering anything approaching old-world elegance. Witton House was built on the banks of the Black Burn on a site which had once been part of the Norman manor of Billington near Whalley. In 1288 it was owned by Geoffrey de Chadderton from whom it passed into the hands of the de Haldelays, Radcliffes, Standishes, Greenfields and, finally, to John Holme who in 1742 gave the estate to the Fieldens. Around 1800 Henry Fielden replaced the old half-timbered hall with an attractive Georgian building. During the Industrial Revolution Henry's son Joseph was a great benefactor of Blackburn.

The Black Burn rises above Oswaldtwistle, its volume was insufficient to cope with industrial and household pollution, and soon it became almost an open sewer. One branch of the Fielden family had a hall on the river bank at Pleasington but the atmosphere around it became so polluted that the family felt obliged to desert it. The Fieldens of Witton, however, held on. They gave substantial sums of money to St Mark's Church on Buncer Lane, below which are the family vaults. By 1947, however, the Fieldens had left the area and Blackburn Corporation bought Witton for £62,000, but only with the aid of £35,000 from Mr R.E. Hart, an eccentric bachelor with an M.A. from Cambridge and who made a fortune from his ropeworks. At his death he left to Blackburn a magnificent collection of coins, books and medieval manuscripts plus a then substantial sum of £10,000 to construct a gallery to display them. What a pity that the town council of the late 1940s were such a bunch of short-sighted incompetents. They failed to find an extra £11,000 to treat the dry rot in Witton House, they failed to spend the £10,000 left by Mr Hart, and only in the late 1980s did his collection go on display. Why oh why did they not repair Witton House and display the collection there?

Witton House was demolished, only some of the outhouses remain and in them is centred the administration of the Country Park which has become one of Blackburn's tourist traps. Nature trails lead through woodlands up onto a hilltop covered with bilberry and heather, all that remains of the once extensive and well-managed grouse shoot of the Fieldens. During 1990 we made a television film about the Country Park which now has a small collection of native animals including

Darwen Tower, built to celebrate Queen Victoria's Golden Jubilee.

wood mice, polecats, voles and harvest mice as well as grey squirrel, mink, ferrets and rabbits. The wardens have become very skilled in the difficult art of releasing injured animals such as badgers back into the wild and have also had considerable success in the release of barn owls.

If Blackburn itself lacks an historic house, then this is more than made up for by Hoghton Tower dominating a hill on the Preston Road, and Samlesbury Hall, described in Chapter 11. The tower is open on Bank holidays and Sundays throughout the summer and also on Saturdays during July and August.

The de Hoghtons have been in occupation since the Norman Conquest but the present tower overlooking the River Darwen was built during the sixteenth century. Within is one of the most famous banqueting halls in the world, for it was here in 1617 that King James I was entertained at great expense by the de Hoghtons. James was so delighted with the quality of his steak that he drew his sword and knighted the beef – thus we have the origin of Sirloin beef, a fact commemorated in the name of the local inn.

Just beyond Hoghton is Brindle Bar, an old toll house on the crossroads between the old routes to Blackburn and Leyland. On the way to Leyland is the ancient village of Brindle. In 1990 Brindle Church celebrated its 800th anniversary, and although it is now dedicated to St James, its original saint was actually Helen who was usually associated with springs or wells. It is quite probable that the original settlement sprang up around a reliable supply of fresh water. Inside the church there is some attractive twentieth-century stained glass, but in the Cavendish Arms inn directly opposite the church is some that is older. The building dates to at least 1775 and the windows record details of the Cavendish family whose main base was at Holker Hall in Cumbria but who owned much land in these parts. They are closely related to the Dukes of Devonshire.

From Brindle there is an attractive walk across fields to Withnell Fold, an industrial village dominated by a huge chimney. The mill overlooking the canal was built in 1844 to produce high-quality paper exported to many countries and used to print bank notes. A town trail leaflet is on sale which points out the old reading room, now a private house, the village stocks, and an aqueduct soaring 100 feet (31 metres) above the valley floor which conducts Manchester's water supply on its way from Thirlmere in the Lake District.

Dominating the skyline to the west of Blackburn is Victoria Tower, also called Jubilee Tower, on Darwen Moor, and to reach it involves one of the most attractive strolls in the country. This was always popular with the cotton workers, but since the clean air acts of the 1950s have improved visibility, the views are now always spectacular. Jubilee Tower was constructed to celebrate the Silver jubilee of Victoria's accession in 1837 and stands on top of a 1225 feet (372 metre) hill. The view from the top of the tower, which is always open, is enhanced by plaques indicating the hills seen from it including

Pendle, Great Whernside, Fountains Fell, Penyghent, Ingleborough, Whernside, Burn Fell, Longridge Fell, Fairsnape Fell, the Langdale Pikes, Bowfell, Coniston Old Man, Kinder Scout, Holcolm Fell, Boulsworth, Black Combe, Snaefell on the Isle of Man plus Snowden and the Welsh mountains.

The climb up to the tower from Sunnyhurst with its own impressive visitor centre, cafe and nature trails provides a perfect view of Darwen with the chimney of the India Mill particularly prominent. This was constructed from handmade bricks in the style of the campanile in St Mark's Square in Venice. Some would say that the Lancashire climate if exported would help to fill the canals of Venice, whilst an old worker from Darwen described mill architecture to us as the rain was pouring down: 'If thas gunna build a shed tha' mun as weal do it reet'. In the case of India Mill they did!

Two other mill towns with impressive buildings are Leyland and Chorley. Leyland has retained its connection with the countryside in 160 acres of open park, woodland walks, a children's play area, a better than average cafe, a maze and a miniature railway.

Mention Leyland, even in these days of a depression in British engineering, and the thought of a good old Leyland bus comes to mind. Most towns in the world have had a reliable Leyland at one time or other. On King Street is the British Commercial Vehicle Museum which is open daily except Mondays (unless there is a bank holiday) between April and September but in October and November it only opens at weekends. The exhibits range from horse-drawn vehicles through a fine collection of steam-powered and early petrol and diesel vehicles right up to modern times. Whilst many of Lancashire's museums relate specifically to the history of the county itself, this is one of the most important transport museums in the world. There are good facilities for the disabled.

A third place to visit in Leyland is the Heritage Museum which was the old Grammar School, part of which dates to the late sixteenth century. Here on display are features of the old market town, but what drew our initial attention was a copy of the scorecard of the first-ever test match between England and

Australia which was played at Melbourne. It records that a batsman named Thompson was bowled by Allen Hill for one. Hill came from Chorley Cricket Club which therefore has the distinction of having taken the first-ever test wicket.

Also on display are a set of packhorse bells, probably made in Wigan, and there is a map of the road between London and Carlisle dated 1675 which passed through the centre of Leyland. It was then an important market town and it still has a few buildings to prove this fact including St Andrew's Church, first mentioned in 1055 but most of it dating to the thirteenth century. Almost as old is the Eagle and Child which is said to date to around 1230 and which was important to travellers along the ancient highway.

The Council for the Protection of Rural England has a visitor centre and its headquarters at Worden Park, and there is also an Arts and Crafts Centre. Both are open throughout the year although the CPRE centre closes in January.

As we have seen in Chapter 1, what is now Lancashire was once divided into six areas called hundreds and Leyland, although the smallest of these, was still by far the most important town in this area although it is now overshadowed by Blackburn and especially by Chorley.

Near to Chorley and close to the M6 and M61 motorways at Charnock is the Camelot Theme Park which is an exciting day out for children, but adults are also fascinated by the spectacular falconry displays which are a feature during the season.

Anyone approaching modern Chorley and observing the strenuous efforts being made to get a Lancashire New Town off the ground can be forgiven for failing to recognise it as an old market centre. Although records of the original market charter have been lost, it is known that Chorley was once the only market town in the hundred of Leyland, but the official records take us back only to 1498. Originally Chorley – set on the river Chor and a tributary of the Yarrow which itself feeds the Douglas-Ribble complex – was ecclesiastically governed from Croston where a magnificent church is set close to a packhorse bridge and looks more like a cathedral than a parish church.

In its turn Chorley was larger and more influential than

Between the wars Leyland buses were running along the streets of most towns in Britain. All models are on display at the museum in the vehicles' home town.

Bolton, its southern neighbour. In 1297, for example, Bolton had only 69 burgages whilst Chorley sported 90. Once set among green meadowlands, Chorley's name derived from 'the field or lea of the churls or husbandmen'. What could be more natural than the development of a market in such a spot? The motto of the town is 'Beware'. No doubt there was plenty to beware of in the old days, but the modern visitor in search of Chorley's market should also beware, for the town has not one market but two!

Each Monday night the huge town-centre car park is closed and stalls are erected to make up what has for some unknown reason become known as the 'Flat Iron Market'. This takes place each Tuesday, whilst the 'normal market' is bustling not only on Tuesdays, but on Fridays and Saturdays as well. The main activity takes place along Market and Chapel Streets. Despite the fact that the M6 and M61 motorways are within easy reach of the town, the fact that the A6 passes along Market Street brings problems of traffic congestion. Plans are afoot to pedestrianise further and build supermarkets in the shopping centre, but many feel that this may rip the guts out of the ancient market place. The covered market with its quaint pantiled roof must be retained if the regular stream of visiting shoppers is to be assured and stallholders' income guaranteed.

Our tour of the town began at the one-time Chorley Technical College with its magnificent 1906 facade which has recently been converted into a spacious library with a friendly reference section which is an ideal spot to find out about famous folk who once lived in Chorley. No one deserves an international reputation more than Miles Standish (1584-1656) who was described in the last chapter.

Close to the library is the parish church, across from which is a Georgian building on Terence Mount, now the Trustee Savings Bank but often said to be the birthplace of Sir Henry Tate (1819-1899), the founder of the sugar firm who provided the finance for London's famous art gallery. Henry's father was the Reverend William Tate, a Unitarian minister in charge of the Dissenter's Chapel. In 1832 young Henry was apprenticed to the grocery trade in Liverpool, so it is only right that in the late 1980s a Tate gallery should have been set up along the edge of the Albert Dock there. The lad must have worked hard in Liverpool because by 1839 he had set himself up in his own business. By 1855 he had six shops, and it must have caused Henry many a sleepless night before he sold his thriving business in order to raise capital to enter the already competitive sugar market. It took great courage to convert his new sugar factory to take modern refining machinery from France, but this eventually enabled him to corner the British market and make a fortune. Always a generous man, Henry Tate gave away vast sums of money to worthy causes.

Across from Tate's probable birthplace is the grand old church of St Lawrence which still retains an atmosphere of village tranquility. A stroll around the exterior reveals a fine beech hedge, and a steep view down to the ancient hostelry called the 'Swan with Two Necks'. The building dates back to 1790, but was a private dwelling until the late 1970s when it became a pub.

St Lawrence's is the oldest building in Chorley and stands on the site of a Saxon chapel, but the present building is mainly of fifteenth-century construction. Why is the church dedicated to St Lawrence? In the fifteenth century a church with a goodly supply of saintly relics could extract a workable income from hopeful pilgrims. James Standish of Duxbury in 1442 gave the saint's relics to the rector of Croston, who allowed them to be enshrined in Chorley Church. Sir Richard is said to have brought these remains back from Normandy. They may have been originally obtained by Sir Rowland Standish who was killed in a battle in Picardy in 1435.

The interior of the church has many reminders of the Standish family which have been retained despite substantial, but most probably necessary, alterations, enlargements and refurbishments during the period 1859-1861 and again in 1914.

Astley Hall, one of the finest houses in the county, can be reached from the town centre off the main A6, and a footpath winds its way through peaceful wood and parkland full of birds and flowers. The house, dating to the sixteenth and seventeenth centuries, overlooks a pond attractive to wildfowl, and the entrance opens out into a magnificently airy hall decorated with portraits. Astley has a fine collection of furniture including a 23½-foot-long shovel table and a bed said to have been occupied by Oliver Cromwell at the time of the Battle of Preston in 1648. There is also a pair of his boots.

The drawing room has a ceiling decorated with scenes from the story of the Golden Fleece. In an upper room is a fine art gallery, and often on summer Sunday afternoons the lady guides are dressed in Tudor costume, which adds to the lovely atmosphere of the place.

Returning to the town from Astley, especially at midday with the Flat Iron Market in full steam, will relate Chorley's tale to perfection as the characteristics of an industrial town of the cotton age are blended with those of a long-established market centre. Leland, writing in 1536, thought that Chorley had 'a wonderful poor or rather no market'. By 1790 it was described as 'a small neat market town'. Just where the first market was held is by no means certain but the original site and the cross which was surrounded by steps may have been destroyed during the construction of the new Town Hall between 1875 and 1879. The market rights were held by the Lord of the Manor, and during the nineteenth century the powerful Gillibrand family would have had every right to build on the green. Supporting this theory is the fact that the town hall is close to the parish church. As stagecoach traffic built up during the nineteenth century, traffic congestion must have been an increasing problem. Near the river at Red Bank was the Yarrow Bridge Hotel, a coaching house mentioned by Thomas de Quincey (1785-1859) who was born and educated in Manchester and wrote *Confessions of an English Opium Eater*, published in 1822. Thomas Gillibrand provided a new market place in 1826. Then, as now, the main market was held on a Tuesday, but is certain that on at least two other days each week fish was brought from the sea and also from long-established fisheries along the Ribble, to be first washed under a pump and laid out for inspection on the fish stones. In 1874 the local authority took over the manorial rights on payment of £5500, and after the removal of large numbers of old cottages a paved and almost totally covered market was created. Not all stallholders were pleased with the facilities and a shooting gallery was a particular bone of contention. In 1885 a pillar gas lamp was erected to provide the 'light of security' for stallholders. By this time Chorley had its 'rough element' as young mill workers looked for distractions after a hard day's work. The change from agriculture to textiles can be seen by looking at a map of 1769 when the present Market Street is described as 'the highway from Chorley Moor to Chorley

Splendid woodland walks run through Darwen's Sunnyhurst Woods.

Cross'. Handloom weaving provided agricultural workers of the surrounding area with much-needed extra income and they were far from pleased when Arkwright imported new and very efficient spinning machinery into his mill at Birkacre. From a peaceful agricultural town the Birkacre riots dragged Chorley into the worst of the civil unrest generated by the Industrial Revolution.

The area around Birkacre has now been laid out as a nature reserve, yet another example to prove that not all the pessimism of modern-day conservationists is justified. Lancashire is the living proof of the rule that nature can survive whatever the problems that beset her.

CHAPTER 9

Burnley and the Calder Valley

Mention the River Calder to residents of Todmorden on the border with Yorkshire, and they will say 'Which one?' The Yorkshire Calder heads for its union with the River Aire and thence to the Humber estuary on the east coast whilst the Lancashire Calder, whose source is close by, flows westwards to meet the Ribble near Whalley and thence to the coast via Preston and Southport. In this chapter we follow the river from its source to the charming village of Whalley.

The Lancashire Calder, before coal was discovered in plenty all around Burnley and until the cotton came, was full of trout and salmon and had magnificent manor houses overlooking the valley. Fortunately most of these houses still stand although only two – Towneley and Gawthorpe – are regularly open to the public.

The first house on the journey from Todmorden is at Holme-in-Cliviger which now serves as an old people's home, but the extensive woodlands which surround it have recently been brought back under control in a scheme funded by the local authorities. By the mid-1990s the area should look much as it did to Dr Thomas Dunham Whitaker, the historian who wrote voluminously about Whalley, Craven and Richmondshire, Whitaker's works were illustrated by the famous painter Turner.

Whitaker was responsible in 1787 for the demolition of an old chantry chapel which gave its name to Holme Chapel in the parish of Cliviger, and in its stead rose St John's Church which was consecrated in 1787. Whitaker himself was vicar here from 1796 to 1821. He seems to have used this grand little church as a private museum; he brought with him a wooden pulpit, apparently from Kirkstall Abbey, and it is thought it may have been situated in the dining room in order that the brethren could be educated as well as fed. There are also a couple of pews from Whalley Abbey and a beautifully carved screen on the east wall which may be yet another example of 'Whitaker's Whalley Collection'.

There is also an interesting 'collection' in the churchyard. We have all heard of the fateful Charge of the Light Brigade on October 25th 1854 during the Crimean War. Fewer folk know that the Heavy Brigade also charged on that day and were much more successful. Their charge was led by General James Scarlett whose home was at Bank Hall House in Burnley. The General's tomb marked by a stone cross is situated close to the church door and a service is held to his memory each year on the Sunday nearest to the battle anniversary.

Opposite the church is the Ram Inn, and here every September is held the Lonk sheep fair, this being a breed peculiar to this area, and among the judges of the dog trials is our friend and local naturalist, Eric Halsall, who gained fame with Phil Drabble in the 'One Man and His Dog' television series.

Trade at the Ram improved once the turnpike road was driven through the valley, and there is a milestone set into the wall between Holme Hall and St John's church. The older road used by the packhorses leads up from the church onto the Long Causeway, the ancient route between Lancashire and Yorkshire. The passage of animals along these old roads wore a deep trough and they were often known as hollow ways – it is highly likely that this is how London's Holloway got its name.

The turnpike of the late eighteenth century also brought the remote but historic hamlet of Hurstwood a little nearer civilisation. Some believe that in A D 937 the bloody battle of Brunenburn was fought here in which the Saxons defeated the Danes, but the precise site will probably never be known. What is beyond dispute is that here flows the River Brun, a tributary of the Calder, from which Burnley (Brun-lea) takes its name and that there is a so-called battle stone close to Hurstwood village. In the settlement itself are three buildings of note, the Elizabethan Hurstwood Hall, Spenser's House which is also Elizabethan, and Tattersall's Tenement, which is possibly the oldest of the three.

Edmund Spenser, author of *The Faerie Queen* which so pleased Elizabeth I, is said to have spent some time in his relatives' cottage in Hurstwood. Positive proof, however, is lacking. Searching through his writings, especially *The Shepherd's Kalendar*, there seems to be more than a trace of

Lonk Fair, Cliviger.

Lancashire dialect and words which could only have come from contact with northerners. This makes it more than possible that he fell in love with Rose Dyneley, a relative of the Towneleys, but she did not return his love, so young Spenser responded by writing *The Faerie Queen*. Being a good politician, however, he dedicated it to the Queen.

There is much more solid evidence regarding Richard Tattersall who left the Hurstwood stables, which are still in use today, and entered the service of the Duke of Kingston. He was so succesful that in 1766 he raised the cash to set up the Tattersall Horse Sales in Knightsbridge, and this started a tradition which is still famous throughout the horse-racing world.

Beyond Cliviger the Calder weaves its way towards Burnley, but first passing close to one of the finest houses in the county.

At Towneley there are woodland walks, marine and freshwater aquaria, a natural history centre and a fine craft and industry museum, all based on the early fifteenth century Hall which hosts exhibitions as well as the regular displays in the art gallery and in the craft and industry museum.

Burnley residents know that all these riches cost absolutely nothing. We had the joy during the 1970s of living in a cottage

A substantial cross in the churchyard at Cliviger marks the grave of General Scarlett who led the charge of the Heavy Brigade in the Crimea conflict.

in the wooded grounds, and yet there are nooks and crannies in the Hall and dells in the woodlands which still surprise us.

The Hall can be traced back to feudal England of around 1200. The present building with walls six feet thick was built around 1350, but succeeding generations of the Towneley

Tattersall's Tenement at Hurstwood.

family added to their lands and embellished their home. The menfolk were renowned for their exploits in battle and until the State and Church came into conflict the Towneleys were influential. From the time of Henry VIII, however, the family loyalty to the Catholic faith brought them nothing but trouble. John Towneley (1528-1607) spent 25 years in prison and was only released when he was blind and too old to be considered a threat. Colonel Francis Towneley (1709-1746) fared even worse and was executed for his part in Bonnie Prince Charlie's rebellion, His severed head was kept at the Hall until 1947 when it was laid to rest in the family vault in St Peter's Church in Burnley which in 1990 was given a much needed facelift.

The Towneleys were never to achieve high office because of their faith – this was the nation's loss. Surely the bravery of the family could have been put to better use than constructing illicit chapels and priest holes. However, the best-known member of the family made his mark in the arts rather than in politics. This was Charles Towneley (1737-1805), whose collection of classic sculpture was so renowned that the British Museum purchased it after his death and constructed the Towneley Gallery. The family were no doubt delighted in 1828 with the passing of the Catholic Emancipation Act when

Spenser's House, Hurstwood.

Peregrine Towneley became High Sherrif of Lancashire, a postition also held by his son, colonel John Towneley. The estate at this time was justly famous for its stockbreeding. Master Butterfly was a champion bull in 1856 and was sold for a record sum, but in 1861 the horse breeders had even more cause for celebration when Kettledrum won the Derby at 16-1 and many local folk made a great deal of money. Two local hostelries, the Butterfly and the Kettledrum, celebrate these events.

Just when the animal-breeding programme reached its peak, the family itself ran out of males. Lieutenant Richard Henry Towneley died only a few months before his father, the brother of Charles Towneley, who himself had been at the Hall only for a matter of weeks. The 40,000 acre estate had to be divided by an Act of Parliament among six co-heiresses, and Towneley Hall was given to Lady O'Hagan, Charles' youngest daughter, who is buried at St John's in Cliviger. This generous lady (1846-1921), finding the Hall something of a financial burden, still sold it at a most reasonable price to Burnley Corporation, and it opened as an Art Gallery and Museum on 28 May 1903. The family, however, are still intact and influential. Lord O'Hagan is a member of the European

One of the world's most unusual sundials set up outside Marsden Hall in 1841.

Parliment, Simon Towneley who lives close to Towneley at Barcroft is Lord Lieutenant of Lancashire, and Peregrine Worsthorne is famous in the world of journalism. None of the family, past or present, could have anything but praise for what has happened to their ancestral home since it became one of Burnley's proudest possessions.

So much for Towneley, but what about Burnley itself? It is difficult to write without bias about the town where one shops and goes for entertainment and to watch the football team. If we shop at Sainsburys we cannot miss the huge limekilns which have been left in the car park and marked by a plaque. Above the kilns is a straight stretch of the Leeds to Liverpool Canal known as 'the straight mile', and here lime was unloaded. It was converted into cement which was vital at a time when mills and houses were being built in large numbers.

It is possible to walk the canal towpath to the Weaver's Triangle Visitors' Centre which is open between April and September and at other times by appointment. The small museum is sited in the canal toll house and contains displays

Marsden Hall in 1905.

devoted to the canal and the cotton industry – hence the Weaver's Triangle, for Burnley specialised in the weaving as against the spinning of cotton. On the outskirts of the town is Queen's Mill at Harle Syke which is a combination of working mill and museum. The opening times are variable but details can be obtained from the Mechanics' Institute Information Centre close to the town hall in the town centre, some of which was pedestrianised in 1990. At Queen's Mill there is a huge steam engine called 'Peace' which does not sound anything like it as it drives the looms. These weave union shirting, and it is possible to buy the mill products in the shop.

These days it is not possible to separate Burnley from Nelson and Colne which share a valley running almost at right angles to the Calder.

Nelson is a modern textile town named after the Lord Nelson Hotel close to the railway line running along the valley bottom. Two suburbs above the town called Little and Great Marsden are of ancient origin and Marsden Park is on these lands. Marsden Hall was the home of the de Walton family until they ran out of heirs in 1912 when the local authority

Gawthorpe Hall, Padiham, one-time home of the Shuttleworth family and open to the public.

took over. During the development of the park part of the Hall was demolished, but a substantial portion was retained and is now an Italian restaurant. Close by is a unique sundial erected in 1841 which attracts visitors from all over the world. There are pointers which tell the time in many parts of the world including Fort Nelson USA, Jerusalem, Calcutta, Buenos Ayres, Moscow, London, Hermits Isles, St Pedro, Cape Isabella, Rome St Helena, and Adams Park Ceylon (now Sri Lanka).

There is a lovely old road leading from Marsden to Colne which, until the valley was developed, was a market town specialising in wool. Although much of the centre has been spoiled by development, St Batholmew's Church, founded in

The gatehouse and courthouse at Martholme Hall. Now privately owned, the recently restored house was once the stately home of the Fittons and Heskeths, whose main residence was at Rufford near Southport. Martholme is thought to have been the site of an ancient market, and the court house bears witness to its one-time importance. Photograph taken in 1905.

Altham Church is one of the finest in the district, and since the closure of local coal mines the Calder which flows around it is much clearer.

1122, is still a joy with lots of interesting furnishings. Time should also be spared to investigate more modern history in the form of a statue to Lawrence Hartley, who was the brave bandmaster of the *Titanic* who went on conducting as the ship sank on her maiden voyage in 1912.

Returning to Burnley and following the Calder, the next stop should be at Gawthorpe Hall, a real rival to Towneley, where in the 1960s we were often entertained by Miss Racheal Kay-Shuttleworth the last in a line of private owners going back to the fourteenth century. The splendidly proportioned hall is sited on a bluff overlooking a sweeping bend of the river. In 1559 an extensive rebuilding took place around the original pele tower which once guarded an important ford over the river. The Hall is open to the public between April and October, but it is also used by Nelson and Colne College which organises a number of fascinating courses especially in household crafts such as embroidery and needlework which so fascinated Miss Rachael throughout her long life. The Hall is now owned by the National Trust.

The meandering Calder on its way to the Ribble squeezes its way between Padiham power station and Mullards television factory and twists around the ancient church at Altham. On the opposite bank are the halls of the Starkies at Huntroyd near Simonstone and the Nowells at Read.

Huntroyd Hall is still in the hands of the Starkie family who have held it since it was a hunting lodge owned by the Plantagenet kings. Extensive rebuilding was carried out in 1576 and in 1633; it is said that Inigo Jones (1573-1652) played his part in the present design.

Read Hall which is also privately owned has not maintained its connection with its original owners and at one time seemed destined to become a leisure centre. The Nowells were one of Lancashire's most famous families and it was Roger Nowell who in 1612 committed the Lancashire witches for trial (see Chapter 10). Alexander Nowell (1507-1602), however, played his part on the national stage and was no mere parochial actor.

Although he rose to be Dean of St Paul's, Alexander frequently annoyed Elizabeth, but when he sensed danger he escaped into the country – he may even have returned to Read Hall – and went fishing. It is said that he once left a flagon of ale in a stream to cool, and after being called away in a hurry he returned a few days later to find his ale frothy and bitter tasting. Bottled beer was born!

The Hall, however, passed out of the hands of the Nowells in 1772 and in 1799 it was completely rebuilt in glorious Georgian style; its present appearance is a tribute to Webster, the Kendal-based architect.

Another ancient and privately owned hall is the sixteenth-century Martholme which has recently been restored, but alas Moreton Hall sited down in a dip near the river below the Whalley Road was demolished above thirty years ago. A house was built on the site of a previous hall in 1829, and apparently it had 365 windows and 52 chimneys. After a period of use by Polish military personnel during the last war its upkeep was considered too high and down it came. Its grounds are still visible to the left of the road into Whalley just before the sign to Spring Wood appears on the right.

We wonder if Spring Wood near Whalley got its name from the lovely clear water which trickles through its wooded cloughs, or because of how delightful it is when smothered beneath a colourful tangle of spring flowers. We decided to

Whalley Church is even older than the nearby Abbey.

accept the former because this is a wood for all seasons and should not just belong to one season. In autumn the fungi include the red and white fly agaric which thrive under the birches.

A circular walk passes through the woodlands, and as the path descends into the picnic area there is a footpath which crosses a stile and passes under the road. The path then descends through lush green fields hedged by hawthorns and flanked by streams. As we crossed a stile our dog was slightly in front of us, and as he sat waiting for us to cross the stile his movement disturbed the vegetation and produced a strong smell of aniseed. There we found the white flowers and fern-like leaves of sweet cecily, a relative of the carrot and a member of the family Umbelliferae.

After passing through a group of lovely old cottages, the track reaches the Whalley to Clitheroe road at the junction of the Mitton Road at which stands the old Whalley Grammar School with a war memorial in front of it. A left turn through the village leads to Whalley church, and beyond this is the Abbey. The parish church is thirteenth century, but within the churchyard are three more ancient crosses.

Although looking around churches is a suitable diversion in cool, windy and wet weather, the interior of Whalley Church should never be missed. Here is a set of the finest choir stalls to be found anywhere. These were originally eighteen in number, but six more have been added, so now they total twenty-four. They were brought here, in the reign of Queen Mary, from the Abbey after its destruction in 1537, and have occupied this sacred spot ever since. They are made of the finest English oak, and though not finely adorned in the upper parts, they are curiously carved in the lower parts. For instance, on the Prior's stall is a very laughable sculpture of a satyr, covered with long hair, and armed with a club, in a posture of supplication, and weeping tears of oak at the feet of a buxom girl who is evidently laughing at his suit.

On another appears a grave, strong man, with his sword and buckler thrown away, kneeling in utter subjection before a female, who is practising the principles of home rule by beating him on the head with a frying pan. A third stall bears a carving of a man shoeing a goose, and an inscription:

> Whoso telles him of what another does
> Let him come here and shoe the goose.

Although the origins of Whalley Abbey go back to 1172, it did not begin at Whalley but on the banks of the River Mersey at Stanlow, where now stands a huge oil refinery. In 1296 the monks had found the environment so tough that they negotiated a move to Whalley on a much more fertile stretch of land close to the River Calder. Again though, trouble was never far from this group of Cistercians because the site at Whalley was so close to the existing abbey at Sawley. The latter feared competition in persuading local folk to donate land and goods 'for the good of their souls'. It was not until 1310 that the Whalley monks felt secure enough to start building, but once things got under way the abbey quickly took shape, and by 1400 a delightful structure was raised, much more imposing than that at Sawley. It is therefore easy to see why the two abbeys never lived easily together.

Life at Whalley seems to have been fairly tranquil until Henry VIII, from 1536 onwards, began to dissolve the monasteries. The King, however, did not anticipate the depth of religious feeling in the North of England and was caught off guard in 1536 when many abbeys took part in the revolution known as the Pilgrimage of Grace. For the first time the abbots of Sawley and Whalley spoke with one voice, and both men perished as Henry took revenge upon those who opposed him. Many abbeys, including Sawley, were torn down (see Chapter 11).

The best memorial to Abbot Paslew who was responsible for creating an abbey of great beauty at Whalley is not his supposed grave in the churchyard, but his house, the site of which has been in continual use since the Dissolution. The lands and buildings were purchased by the Assheton and Bradyll families and the abbot's lodgings were rebuilt as a family home for the former. It passed into the Curzon family by marriage but the direct Assheton link remained until 1830. The building has been owned and lovingly cared for by the Diocese of Blackburn since 1923 and functions as a conference centre. Few such places have such a friendly atmosphere for and Abbot Paslew's soul must feel some degree of peace and happiness at the turn of events.

The Calder flows on past the Abbey and beneath the arches of a red brick aqueduct carrying the railway line between Blackburn and Clitheroe. At the confluence of the Calder with the Ribble stands yet another ancient house of distinction – Hacking Hall, where almost within living memory a rowboat ferry known as Hacking Boat crossed the river. Although it is now a farmhouse, Hacking once belonged to the family of Judge Walmesley whose main home was at Dunkenhalgh, now a fine hotel situated just off the M65 motorway between Burnley, Blackburn and Accrington. It is a good place for visitors to Lancashire to use as a base.

CHAPTER 10

Bowland and Pendle

On either side of the River Ribble lie the Bowland Fells and Pendle Hill. Bowland has some lovely villages but until recently it had been a difficult place to walk as there are so many restricted areas and badly marked footpaths. But things are improving. Pendleside also has its problems, the main one being its association with the witchraft trials of 1612. This, especially at Hallowe'en, can result in too many people in too little space. On the whole, though, even the witches' village of Roughlee where we now live remains a place of peace and tranquility.

The main river draining the Bowland fells is the Hodder which is unpolluted along its whole length and is one of the best salmon rivers in England, joining the Ribble near Whalley. In 1988 we made a film on the river with the late Russell Harty just before his death. There was nobody like Russell for prising secrets out of people: who else could have persuaded a tough gamekeeper to admit that he had actually seen a flying saucer? He told of the event with such charm that we just had to believe him.

Almost all of Lancashire has changed out of recognition since the Norman Conquest; Bowland is the exception. Locals pronounce the area as Bolland and well know why it has been declared an Area of Outstanding Natural Beauty. This was part of the extensive lands of the Saxon Earl Tostig and it was such good hunting country that the Normans always keen on their sport, soon took over. It is still reasonably easy to find the old boundaries. In the early days there were many more trees but this was never a dense forest – which would have made it impossible for hunting – but an area of small farms and scattered trees ideal for enjoying a good chase. Once the Royal forests were established, only the king and his favourites could hunt game, and there were courts at Slaidburn to try those who broke the forest laws.

Once the modern counties began to evolve, Bowland was in

Wheatear.

Yorkshire, whilst once the steep road known as the Trough was climbed, the traveller was in Lancashire. Since the boundary changes of 1974 both sides have been in Lancashire. The Hodder drains the eastern fells, whilst the western slopes are the catchment areas for the River Wyre which flows to the sea at Fleetwood. The old boundary marker known as the Grey Stone of Trough stands at the summit, although it only dates to 1897 and replaced a much more ancient indicator.

There was a Roman road running through Bowland which was routed over Longridge Fell, forded the River Hodder to the west of the pretty little village of Newton and then went over sweeping fells to Lowgill. In the Middle Ages the east-west route became more important than the Roman north-west route. This was because the Cistercian abbeys of Whalley and Sawley (see Chapters 9 and 11) needed the port of Lancaster to conduct the business which made them prosperous. This is the origin of the present narrow twisting road over the Trough, and it was this route which was followed by John Paslew, the last Abbot of Whalley, on his way to stand trial following the Pilgrimage of Grace uprising in 1536. Not too long afterwards, in 1612 the Pendle witches followed the same path to their grizzly fate at Lancaster Castle.

Few river sources are so dramatic as that of the Hodder. Whenever we stand at the Cross of Greet close to the source, we are assured of good birdwatching with summer sightings of nesting wheatears guaranteed plus goodly numbers of red grouse, skylark and meadow pipit. In winter the area is hunted by many short-eared owls and a few pairs remain to breed. At one time the Hodder meandered its way between farms and through a village, but these now lie beneath a reservoir.

The 344 acres (130 hectares) of sheltered water formed by the damming of the River Hodder and flooding the tiny hamlet of Dale Head created Stocks Reservoir which is something of a Mecca for northern birdwatchers. The North West Water Authority administer the reservoir which is surrounded by 4000 acres (1600 hectares) of conifers constituting Gisburn Forest under the control of the Foresty Commission. Footpaths have now been laid out from the car park from which there are excellent views over the water. A grassy island, so popular with breeding birds especially black headed gulls and Canada geese, was once a hill overlooking the village. Dale Head was actually visible during the drought of 1976 but usually the buildings are deep under the surface, St James' Church was reconstructed on the banks of the reservoir.

Slaidburn is an attractive village famous for its inn. It stands at the confluence of the River Hodder with its substantial tributary Croasdale Beck, and the visitor is thus treated to the pleasure of two graceful bridges and a network of footpaths following the watercourses. The main car park is close by a green area overlooking the Hodder and the steep main street leads past a war memorial and horse trough to the centre of the village where you find the shop and two old pubs, the Black Bull and the Hark to Bounty. The former no longer serves

Short-eared owls are resident around the catchment area of the Hodder.

alcohol and is in use as a youth hostel, but the Hark to Bounty is one of the most famous inns in the north of England. Until 1861 it was simply called 'The Dog' but it is said that in that year the Master of the Hunt was having a rest and a bite to eat. Outside he heard his favourite hound barking loudly in its impatience to return to the hunt, and the Master said, 'Hark to Bounty', after which the name stuck.

Whilst taking part in the television programme with Russell Harty, we were allowed to spend some time in a room above the bar of the hotel which is accurately referred to as the Court Room. Slaidburn was once the focal point for the administration of justice in the upper Hodder Valley. When the ancient Court House showed signs of age, the judiciary transferred to the Bounty. This was once the only courtroom between York and Lancaster and was in use until 1937. The huge beamed room still has its old benches whilst the dock has been converted into a dispensary for drinks, adding new meaning to the phrase 'called to the bar'. There are two further reminders of the old court house – a studded window composed of coloured glass at the rear of the house, thought to be part of the old building, and Court House Close, now only a field.

Slaidburn is indeed an ancient settlement and the name means a sheep field overlooking a river, and there is plenty of evidence of an Anglo-Saxon presence in the form of cultivation field terraces overlooking the parish church of St Andrew. The tower is so strongly built that it is easy to appreciate that it served as a refuge for the population of the area when the Scots invaded in 1322. Next to the church is the Grammar School bearing a stone with the date 15 May 1717 inscribed upon it. This tells us that a local farmer named John Brennand provided the money for the building which is still used, with an extension, by the local Junior School.

After passing through Newton and Dunsop Bridge, both attractive villages, the Hodder reaches Whitewell. This delightful section of the river set in a wooded gorge overlooked by spectacular hills has rightly earned its name of 'Little Switzerland' and the scenery, as well as the cuisine of the Inn, is well known to walkers, cyclists and motorists throughout the county. Once set deep in the heart of the Forest of Bowland, much of the business of the area was controlled from Whitewell, and in 1400 Walter Urswyck was the keeper. The old church, dedicated to St Michael the Archangel, was once a chapel of ease where bodies were held overnight prior to being interred at Clitheroe. The Reformation which took place around 1540 resulted in the abandonment of the Clitheroe chapel, and the moneys once given to that establishment were diverted to Whitewell. The chapel was enlarged in 1818, but part of the fifteenth-century building is still recognisable, notably the boilerhouse window which is a fine example of the Perpendicular style. Inside on the south wall is a beautifully worked tapestry showing the Descent of Jesus from the Cross based on a Rubens picture hanging in Antwerp Cathedral.

Walter Urswyck's manor house was situated next to the chapel, which also served as a court house. In front of the

Whitewell about 1950. It has hardly changed at all since.

house was the old market place where the locals met to exchange gossip, lay in provisions and sell their produce. This manor house dating to 1400 has now been incorporated into the structure of the present inn. Then, as now, the Whitewell served as the focal point for local Bowlanders and travellers through these parts. Visitors are also well catered for, especially anglers who find the stretch of water owned by the hotel provides exciting game fishing. Grayling can be caught between 1st November and 16th March, and this is proving increasingly popular along with fishing for brown and sea trout and salmon.

The Hodder Valley is rightly famous as walking country, and from a wide choice one of our favourites leads to Fairy Holes Caves. From the hotel the route passes the gates of Whitewell Chapel and then down to the right and through a gate into a field. A stile then leads to the river which is shallow and fringed with shingle at this point. Except in flood the river can be crossed here and the path followed to New Laund Farmyard. From here a minor path is followed and climbs steeply to a limestone outcrop which is pock-marked by a system of large and small caves. The largest and most important cave of the system measures 65 feet long by 6 feet wide and 6 feet high (20 metres × 2 metres × 2 metres). It leads into a blocked area which was once used as living accommodation. In 1946 Reginald Mussun carried out an excavation and found a number of bones of animals dating back to the Bronze Age. He also found a shaped pebble which had been used to smash bones in order to get at the marrow inside. A few years ago a hollow stone was found in the river which has been named the 'Whitewell stone', and it may well date to the same period. It is thought to have been used as a mortar, possibly for grinding corn. The Fairy Holes finds can be viewed at Clitheroe Castle Museum (see Chapter 11).

Another unspoiled woodland walk is along the river from the Higher Hodder to the Lower Hodder Bridge, a few yards beyond which is an old packhorse bridge affectionatly known to the locals as Cromwell's Bridge. The walk from the Lower to the Higher Bridge can easily be done in an hour, but we always prefer to take our time and then pause for refreshment at the Hodder Bridge Hotel which overlooks the Higher Bridge.

The so-called Cromwell's Bridge was built by Sir Richard Shireburn at a cost of £70 in 1562, and previous to this time there may well have been another packhorse bridge built to avoid crossing the ford. It is more than likely that Cromwell's army used this ford in August 1648, and the Protector himself may well have crossed the narrow span of the bridge on his way to and from the Shireburns' mansion at Stonyhurst where he was billeted overnight. The old span is best viewed from the new bridge which carries the road from Whalley to Longridge. About a mile further along this road is the village of Hurst Green.

Apart from the modern cars parked outside the Shireburn Arms hotel, the scene has changed little since the 1950s. Adjacent are three vintage petrol pumps which must intrigue visitors, especially those from the big city whose sons attend Stonyhurst College, one of the foremost Roman Catholic Public Schools in the country. The school was once the stately home of the Shireburn family.

From the hotel a gentle stroll takes us past the Shireburn alms houses which have a most fascinating history. They are reached by a flight of steps screened by balustrades and look as if they have been in place for centuries. This is not the case,

Stonyhurst – One of Britain's finest public schools. The 19th century poet Gerard Manley Hopkins taught here.

however, since the alms houses were removed stone by stone in the 1940s from the nearby hill of Kemple End, having outlived their purpose and having been purchased by Stonyhurst College to house their employees.

We cannot complain that the alms houses were uprooted since they would never have been so beautifully restored if they had not been put to good use. The walk continues up a slight incline and around a bend when the true glory of Stonyhurst is revealed.

Stonyhurst must be regarded as an initially tragic house, built by the staunchly Catholic Shireburn family. In 1702 a fine new mansion was in the process of construction when the son and only male heir of Sir Nicholas died after eating yew berries, and the family then lost interest in the house. In 1717, on Sir Nicholas's death, Stonyhurst was inherited by his daughter who was married to the Duke of Norfolk. On her death the house passed to the Weld family who in turn leased it in 1794 to the Jesuits who established their school.

There can be no finer place of learning with grounds provided with ornamental lakes, a fully equipped astronomical observatory and a solidly attractive chapel. Within is one of England's finest libraries which includes a copy of the Lindisfarne Gospel and the prayer book which Mary Queen of Scots took to the scaffold and which contains a pressed lock of her hair.

The list of distinguished old scholars is long and includes Sir Arthur Conan Doyle, Charles Waterton the naturalist and the actor Charles Laughton. The school has occasional open days and also organises summer courses during the holidays.

Another historic house gracing the moorlands of Bowland is Browsholme (pronounced Brews-um). This has been the home of the Parker family since the fourteenth century, the present hall dating from 1507. It is open on Saturday afternoons in June, July and August and at other times by appointment.

The gardens are neat and colourful and the Tudor house, refaced in red sandstone in 1604, contains fine furniture and china. There is also a collection of stained glass removed from Whalley Abbey at its dissolution. Of particualr interest is a gauge once used for measuring dogs to ensure that large animals were not kept by unauthorised owners in an area containing the Royal deer. This dates to the time when the Parkers kept law and order in the Forest of Bowland.

All roads in Bowland seem to lead to Chipping which actually means a market. The village is mentioned in the Domesday Book. Chipping was surrounded by marshland, not at all suitable for building, and so the rocky knoll on which the church now stands was ideally sited for both market and church. The market cross would also have been sited here. Just inside the gate, reached by a flight of stone steps, is a sundial dated 1708 and bearing the initials of the churchwardens at the time. The step on which the sundial stands is thought to be the base of the old cross. The local children know the steps of the church and iron gates to which they lead very well because it is here that they carry out their perrying. As a wedding in the church draws to its close the gates are tied with string and the couple are not allowed to pass through until they throw money down the steps. When the youngsters have scrambled for this they untie the string and the gates creak open.

Unlike Bowland, Pendle is best explored by following a circular route along pleasant roads and passing through a

St. Bartholomew's Church at Chipping, with the 'perrying' gates open.

necklace of pretty villages without ever losing sight of the hill itself. We say 'hill' since at 1,831 feet (558 metres) Pendle is actually 169 feet (51 metres) short of reaching the official 2,000 feet entitling it to be called a mountain. In the late 1980s a well laid out footpath called The Pendle Way was created and can be joined from many of the villages which we are about to describe. A climb to the flat summit reveals all the villages below, plus a panorama of the East Lancashire mill towns and also across to Morecambe Bay. George Fox, the founder of the Quaker movement, climbed the hill in 1652 and wrote in his diary that he was 'moved' to convert the people living below to his way of thinking.

Our 'move' around the hill begins at Downham, so often the winner of Lancashire's Best Kept Village competitions. It is easy to see why when you stand opposite the church of St Leonard, near the Assheton Arms Hotel, and look beyond the stocks overshadowed by a gnarled old sycamore and up to the sinuous curve of Pendle. Downham is still an estate village and has been carefully tended by successive members of the Assheton family whose present head is Lord Clitheroe. The family, however, has influenced other areas of the county including, as we have seen, Ashton-under-Lyme and Middleton. Even Downham's telephone box is painted grey to blend in with the cottages, many of which have mullioned windows and gloriously perfumed gardens.

Summering swallows, house martins and swifts nest under eaves, and sweep for insects over Downham Beck, where visitors gather to feed the resident mallards. Close to the large but unobtrusive car park a narrow but perfectly driveable lane leads to Worston, cutting through an area unchanged since the filming of the classic *Whistle Down the Wind*.

In an issue of the *Rambler* magazine published in May 1906, the writer has this to say about Worston's inn: 'The notable Calf's Head Inn . . . is well known to all pedestrians and cyclists. Here assembled the Mock Corporation of Worston, and elected its sham Mayor, who paid sham debts with prodigious sham cheques, drawn on an equally sham bank. The coat of arms was a picture of a calf's head, accompanying which was a motto stating that 'Brains Will Tell'. In 1989 this amusing ritual was resurrected, and what fun it generated!

Roughlee at the turn of the century.

Behind the Inn on the old Green is a much more serious association with cattle in the form of a bull ring set into a stone. Here the unfortunate animal was tethered prior to being baited by bulldogs which were bred specially for this barbaric sport. Perhaps we are wrong in calling it a sport, but at one time bull-baiting was permitted by law because it was believed that the treatment tenderised the flesh of the beast. These days, however, there is nothing so unpleasant and Worston is one of the most delightful and unspoiled of the Pendle villages.

Nearby is Little Mearley Hall which does not seem to have changed since it was visited by the correspondent of the *Rambler* magazine in May 1905 who wrote: 'Little Mearley Hall is at present in the best condition of all the historic halls on this side of Pendle, but it has somewhat lost many of its ancient features. The south-western wing is the oldest part, and, taken as a whole, it presents a very mixed architectural appearance. Dr. Whittaker says that the bay windows at the eastern end were pilfered from the refectory at Sawley Abbey. There is scarcely any doubt that the windows did come from Sawley. The sculptured arms in the panels reveal the Percy coat, and that is sufficient to identify it with the Abbey'.

The walk from Little Mearley towards Worston always sets us wondering why Great Mearley is not now so great. Looking at the humps and bumps on the fields around the two Mearleys

Barrowford Toll House, now restored and occasionally open as a museum.

certainly suggests the presence of an ancient and now 'lost village'. Did it suffer from the plague which was so much a threat during the period from 1380 to 1660s? Perhaps an alternative explanation is to be found by looking up at the towering bulk of Pendle, especially on a day of heavy rain or when the snow is thawing and the meltwater thunders down from the slopes. 'Brasts' or bursts of frightening proportions have been a feature of Pendle. The one of 1669, however, seems to have been the most dramatic: 'The water gushed out near the top of the hill in such quantities and so suddenly that it formed a brast a yard high and continued running for about two hours. It grew unfordable and the houses in Worston two miles from the point of eruption were completely inundated'.

At Pendleton the Swan with Two Necks hardly differs from the days of around 1772 when it was built as a Royal Mail coaching house. The present A59 road, less than a quarter of a mile away, did not exist then and the coaches would have

Higherford Bridge is one of the most impressive packhorse bridges in the country.

trundled through the village, which was mentioned in the Domesday Book.

From Pendleton a steep road climbs up to the Nick of Pendle from which there are splendid views and on which is situated the Wells Springs Hotel, famous throughout the county for its dry ski slopes. There are also several ideal 'lauching pads' from which intrepid hang gliders hurl themselves into space.

From the Nick the road descends into Sabden, once a flourishing textile village which has gradually become a quiet backwater. The church of St Nicholas, although only built in 1841, looks much older and is surrounded by colourful masses of rhododendrons and azaleas framing splendid views over the valley to Padiham Heights where there is a neat little picnic site.

A narrow road leads via Sabden Fold into witch country, dominated by Newchurch-in-Pendle, a quaint, steep, winding village of grey stone dovetailing into the eastern foothills of Pendle. It was once called 'Goldshaw Booth', which means a golden wood (obviously autumnal) with a booth, which was a clearing in which cows were kept. The present name derives from the 'new church' of St Mary which was added around 1740 onto the existing sixteenth-century tower to which a clock was added in 1946. A much older 'eye of God' is carved on the outer wall of the tower, its purpose to ward off evil spirits whilst the faithful were at prayer.

The Lamb Club, 1895.

In the churchyard is the reputed but not proven grave of Alice Nutter of the nearby Roughlee Hall who was one of the ten witches hanged at Lancaster in 1612. Living in Roughlee close to Alice Nutter's fine Tudor mansion, now converted into private housing but still impressive, we often wonder what a fine lady was doing associating with bad-tempered old crones pretending to dabble in the occult to frighten local folk into giving them money.

Alice Nutter was a Catholic who had also just won a land dispute with Roger Nowell of Read Hall. It was Roger, a magistrate, who passed the 'witches' on to higher authority. What was Alice to say? If she had attended mass on Good Friday she would be tortured to reveal the priest and her friends. Far better, we think, to admit to having attended a coven of witches who were going to be hanged anyway. Either way this unhappy lady was doomed, and we think she saved her friends and her priest. It is significant that Roger Nowell got his lands back thereafter!

A seventeenth-century tragedy has proved to be a late twentieth-century bonanza for Newchurch, and the village shop is appropriately called 'Witches Galore'. It is guarded by three life-sized models of wrinkled crones, and an inscription

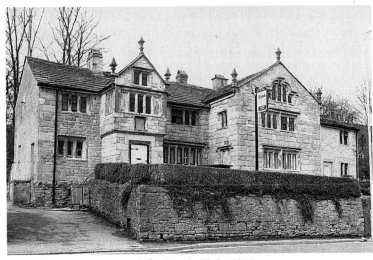

The Lamb Club, 1990.

over the door urges customers not to hang on to their money but 'Gerrit-spent'.

Beyond Newchurch is Barley, washed by Pendle Water and the best starting point for the climb up to Pendle's summit which is marked by a pile of stones called the Beacon. The beacon was lit to celebrate Queen Victoria's Silver Jubilee when all the signal stations were used as in days of old when invasions were a threat.

In Barley there is a large car park, information centre and picnic site beside Pendle Water. From Barley the stream flows on to Roughlee, part of which was once known as Happy Valley. Here were cafes (our house was one and the outside loo still has the penny slot machine) and tea gardens, and an old mill lodge which provided water for the machinery was used for boating and was surrounded by swing boats and other entertainments.

After meandering for a couple of miles across lush meadows, Pendle Water flows through Barrowford and then on through Nelson before bypassing Burnley and joining the River Calder near Gawthorpe Hall in Padiham. It is fitting that this chapter should end at Barrowford, for here is situated the Pendle Heritage Centre. Although it looks like a large industrialised village, Barrowford has four historic buildings and one of the most attractive packhorse bridges in England.

The name of the White Bear Inn is thought to indicate that bear baiting may once have taken place in the area, but there is another possibility. The *White Bear* was a galleon built in 1564 and it was one of Sir Francis Drake's squadron which attacked Cadiz and singed the King of Spain's beard in 1587.

Local historians agree that the White Bear was built for the Hargreaves family using their profits from the cloth trade, and it was first known as 'Hargreaves Great House'. The grounds of the house were disturbed by the construction of the turnpike road. Still standing a few hundred yards from the White Bear and on the junction of the road to Colne stands the Old Tollhouse, now converted into a small museum in association with the Pendle Heritage Centre on the opposite bank of Pendle Water. The Heritage Centre was once the home of the Bannister family, its most famous member – although he never lived here – being Dr Roger, the first man to run a mile in under four minutes. The house has mullioned windows and is rapidly developing into one of the most important and interesting heritage centres in the country. There is a herb garden which gives a good impression of how a seventeeth-century household depended upon a supply of plants, both for the kitchen and the first-aid cupboard.

There is an excellent walk from the White Bear passing the Toll House and then along the main road towards Gisburn, until a bridge on a sharp corner is reached. The route then leads to the left alongside Pendle Water which is soon crossed by one of the most majestic packhorse bridges to be found in the whole of England. It was restored during 1987. The White Bear was still a private residence in 1748 and it gave John Wesley refuge from an angry mob after he had tried to preach a sermon from the packhorse bridge. The White Bear became a hotel in 1803, probably due to the construction of the turnpike road.

The fourth of Barrowford's old houses, again recently restored, is the Lamb working men's club. At one time it looked in great danger of falling down, and it is pleasing to see a piece of Tudor England now repaired and looking spruce.

Above Barrowford runs the Leeds to Liverpool Canal, and

once more much restoration work was carried out in 1990 following an extension to the M65 motorway. Car parking and picnicking areas have been provided around Barrowford locks, and in the summer the area is busy with pleasure boats from Wigan, Chorley, Barnoldswick, Skipton and Leeds. The canal corridor is alive and well, another example of Lancashire's ability to rival Lazarus and rise from the dead. Tourism, however, as we shall see in the final chapter, does bring its problems as well as the perhaps more obvious advantages.

CHAPTER 11

The Ribble Valley to Preston

The Ribble has always had its source in Yorkshire, draining the area of Three Peaks of Ingleborough, Whernside and Penyghent before flowing through Giggleswick and Settle. All this delightful area we described in *Discovering the Yorkshire Dales*. From Settle the river flows westwards to the sea beyond Preston. Since 1974 this area has been within the confines of Lancashire, but prior to this the Ribble was the actual boundary with Yorkshire.

The Ribble also flows between Pendle and Bowland, the two areas described in the previous chapter. This chapter describes a river journey along a narrow valley. We feel, perhaps controversially, that this is the one part of Lancashire which is· most under threat. The rest of this book has, we hope, been a catalogue of the triumph of the environment over industry. The Ribble Valley, however, faces a threat from a very modern industry – tourism. It is a small area and it has one thing to sell – unspoiled beauty. The planners are going to have to take great care that building of hotels and 'theme parks' is selective. One way of doing this is to encourage what previously have been small village inns to modernise their accommodation to absorb tourists. There are signs that this is happening, and so hopefully our pessimism may prove to have been misplaced.

It is therefore quite fitting that we begin our journey down the valley at Gisburn, once in Yorkshire and, according to most of the locals, it still is – quite right too!

If you like English pubs, Italian restaurants and ghosts, then this is the place for you. The Ribblesdale Arms has all these enclosed within its ancient walls. When you realise that it is in the heart of one of Ribblesdale's most attractive villages, then you have perfection.

The inscription over the door tells us that it was built in 1635 by Thomas Lister at a cost of £885. It served (and still serves) as a base for the hunt which so delighted the Lister family who became the Lords of Ribblesdale. Each May there is also an exciting point-to-point meeting held on the outskirts of Gisburn.

The Listers rose from humble beginnings at Arnoldsbiggin close to the modern village. Early in the seventeenth century they were able to construct a house in Gisburne (this time it has an 'e') Park which still stands today and is a private hospital. It is reliably reported that Cromwell rested here whilst en route to the Battle of Preston in August 1648. During the eighteenth century the Listers pleased Royalty by raising troops to fight against Napoleon. Their reward came in 1797 when Thomas Lister became the first Lord Ribblesdale; another Thomas was the 4th and last Earl, and died in 1925. A distinguished soldier himself, Thomas must have been devastated by the death of both sons in the First World War. Thomas also took a great interest in politics, and in the Gladstone administration of 1892 he was a member of the Privy Council. His hobby – indeed the love of his life – was horsemanship. Although, like many landowners of the time, his Lordship spent more time in the South than in the North, the tall lean gentleman with the long nose was a well-loved, or perhaps well-respected, figure in hunting circles. Stag hunters gathered at the building, now the Ribblesdale Arms, where both the horses and the hounds were kept. Their quarry was deer kept in the park and the plentiful brown hare. The remnants of the herd of Sika deer which escaped from the park are still a feature of the area. The pack of hounds which hunt the hare are now stabled between Gisburn and Bolton-by-Bowland.

What have gone for ever are the famous White Cattle, once a feature of Gisburne Park. The origins of this herd are often the subject of heated debate, but it is doubtful if we will ever know for sure. It is a pity that they were not preserved, as were the Chillingham white cattle in Northumberland.

Whilst the grounds of the Hall were used for the pursuit of game and birds, the gamekeepers were active and we have a photograph of a grizzly-looking gamekeeper's gallows on which were exhibited stoats, weasels, crows, moles and birds of prey. the word 'vermin' covered a multitude of sinners in those days!

Like the white cattle and gamekeepers, the Listers of Ribblesdale have now gone and the 4th Earl is remembered by a plaque in Gisburn's delightful little church dedicated to St.

The main street through Gisburn has changed little since this photograph was taken in 1905. The Ribblesdale Arms is on the right just opposite the small horse and cart.

Mary the Virgin. His remains are interred in the family vault and were brought from London to Gisburn by train to Hellifield and from there by road. So ended the association between the family and the village, although the last Lord's sisters, Beatrice and Adelaide Lister, both unmarried, remained at Gisburn until they too died.

No account of the establishment would be complete without mention of Mary the resident ghost! It is said that the maid was raped on the back stairs by her boss and was so disturbed by the experience that she hanged herself from a beam on the top landing. Ever since there have been stories of ghostly footsteps and sightings of a lady in white. Staff tell stories of a six-year-old girl seeing, but without expressing any fear, a lady in white walking through a wall. Resident staff tell of tappings on radiators, lights switching on and off in the middle of the night, and one of the upstairs rooms feeling distinctly cold. We did not believe in ghosts. The landlord took us into the room – we felt chilled and the hairs on our necks stood on end. The family dog came up the stairs, halted outside the room and refused to enter and held his tail between his legs. He knew, and so did we. We were converted. Mary is a friendly soul, but she is still a spirit. The spirits in the friendly bar are much more to our taste. All in all the Ribblesdale Arms is a perfect pub in a perfect village.

Why perfect? Here we have an ancient church, an historic old licensed house, a busy Thursday sheep market and a monthly Sunday market which brings the settlement to life. In the Ribblesdale Arms is one final reminder of Gisburn, enclosed in a niche in the wall of the saloon bar. It is a key to the gates of Gisburne Hall which was kept there by an eighteenth-century warden whose job it was to close the gates at night. As he frequently visited the 'Rib' and got drunk, the key was kept in the same spot so that he didn't lose it!

It is worthwhile making a diversion for about a mile along the road to Nelson to visit the Todber Steam Museum based around a caravan site which has static vans but also caters for tourers. Here are old steamrollers and clanking tractors which the owner frequently takes down into Gisburn for a spin. The museum is open daily between 1st March and 31st October. The chance to listen to the 115-key Verbeek steam organ should on no account be missed.

Back in Gisburn a pretty road leads to the village of Bolton-by-Bowland, passing a bridge which was once the meeting point for otter hunters. Now fortunately this barbaric practice has been outlawed, and what few of these delightful mammals remain in the upolluted river may have a chance to recover.

Bolton-by-Bowland has one small village green with a pair of stocks dominated by The Coach and Horses, and another larger green fringed by mature trees, old stone farms, the old courthouse and cottages and the church of St Peter and St Paul which has been a feature of the village since at least 1190. The present building dates to the fifteenth century and to the time when Henry VI was defeated at the Battle of Hexham in Northumberland on May 15 1464 and was given refuge by Sir Ralph Pudsay.

The church interior includes many memorials to the Pudsay family who lived at the now-demolished Bolton Hall, the gates of which are directly opposite the church. A network of footpaths, however, run through the grounds and some of the outhouses are now private dwellings. Sir Ralph himself is commemorated in a splendid limestone carving in the church. He is shown in full armour, surrounded by his three wives.

The hall and church at Great Mitton, photographed from the bridge over the Ribble.

Near the feet of the first wife are the Roman numerals VI indicating the number of children she bore. The second wife managed only II, but beneath the third is the very impressive figure XVII! The children also appear in the carving, the boys depicted as soldiers, the girls in the costume of the period.

Footpaths and a narrow road lead from Bolton-by-Bowland to Sawley, but the village can also be reached from the main road between Gisburn and Clitheroe. Modern travellers speeding up Sawley Brow (brow means a hill) on the modern A59 often pass by this historic village without a second glance or even sparing time to sit and have a quiet drink or meal in one of the most beautifully sited hostelries anywhere in Britain.

Actually there are three Sawley Brows, the oldest following a circular route around the village and probably following an ancient drove road. This is still the most attractive route, and it can be followed either on foot or by car. It is narrow and steep and must have presented real problems in the days of horse transport. The demand for a better road during the turnpike era must have been irrisistible. The road is now closed but both ends are clearly visible, a chicken farm being situated between them. At the lower level in the village itself is Southport House with a gate close by leading into a farm. Look through the gate and the turnpike road is clearly seen climbing steeply towards another gate at the top of the brow, emerging close to the modern road which now bypasses the village. Looking at the slope of this road, it is no wonder that coach passengers were obliged to alight and walk up the hill to give the horses the chance to reach the top. Many an accident happened here when the brakes on the coaches failed to hold on the downhill route. We have also listened to tales told by motorists of the 1920s and '30s of boiling radiators and clutch and brake failures often resulting in horrendous smashes as they tried to overcome the challenge of Sawley Brow. The modern road is much gentler and cars more reliable than in days gone by.

The centrepiece of the village is the ruined Cistercian abbey. Sawley was a daughter house of Fountains Abbey, which was founded in 1132, and in the year 1147 Benedict the Abbot with twelve monks and other attendants set out to establish the new Abbey at Sawley. It is conjectured that in 1381 the occupants totalled 30, but there were also 50 servants. The Abbots were important enough to be summoned to the House of the Lords during the reigns of Edward I and II.

None of the Abbots at Sawley were men of note. The last was William Trafford. Like Paslew, the last Abbot of Whalley, he took part in the insurrection known as the Pilgrimage of Grace in 1536, and on the failure of this rising he was taken prisoner, tried for treason at Lancaster in 1537, and exeucted. Incidentally, we may mention that the arch spanning the roadway formed no part of the original Abbey but was built out of the remains. The traffic early in the century posed no threat to this narrow arch, but eventually far too many cars collided with the masonry. The bridge was demolished and re-sited in a field a little distant from the Abbey ruins.

The market town which serves these middle reaches of Ribble was Clitheroe. It still has its open market which is a joy to shop in even on a cold wet winter's morning. Market days are Tuesday and Saturday with early closing on Wednesday.

The Clitheroe Castle Museum for which adults are charged a small fee is open from Easter to October and has a wide range of exhibits including the old Hacking Ferry Boat (see Chapter 10) and displays of the history and geology of the town and surrounding area.

One of the fine Shireburn monuments in Great Mitton Church.

Clitheroe is the second oldest borough in Lancashire, after Wigan, and gained its charter in 1147. The Castle was built around this time and is thus older than Lancaster's historic pile. Because Clitheroe Castle was perched on a small outcrop of limestone, the architects had little room for manoeuvre and built the smallest Norman keep in England. It was first held by Roger de Poitou, but soon after its construction the De Lacys took over and held the castle until 1311. In the Civil War, Clitheroe was staunchly Royalist, but the castle survived and was bought by the local authority in 1920 and is now the centrepiece of the park which has an open-air bandstand.

The Castle is set on the higher of two limestone knolls with the parish church of St Mary Magdalen perched on the other. This was established in the thirteenth century but it was rebuilt in the early nineteenth. There was a school in the thirteenth century but the Royal Grammar school was established in 1554, its charter being granted by Mary Tudor. The official charter was mislaid until 1990 when a visit by Queen Elizabeth persuaded our friend Dudley Green, a teacher at the school, to set up a hunt for the document. It turned up in the vaults of a local solicitor's office.

Close to Clitheroe are three bridges over the Ribble at Brungerley, Edisford where there are riverside walks, an indoor swimming pool and a caravan site; and Mitton, the latter separating Little Mitton in Lancashire and Great Mitton once in Yorkshire.

At Great Mitton is the Three Fishes Hotel. The sign of the Three Fishes was the coat of arms of Whalley Abbey and the present hostelry is sited on rich farmland which until the late 1530s belonged to the Cistercian brethren.

The Three Fishes stands on one side of the road and the church dedicated to All Hallows on the other. Within this delightful building are some of the finest relics to be seen in any church in Britain. The authorities have obviously thought about the problem of vandalism and have posted a notice on the gates giving details of where the key may be obtained. The church is always open from 2pm to 5pm on Sundays between April and October. What more could the authorities do than this? All Hallows should not on any account be missed.

The word 'Mitton' comes from the Saxon 'mythe' meaning a

Friar Gate, Preston, around 1905.

farm at the junction of two rivers – a perfect description because it is close by that the Hodder feeds into the Ribble. The parish was large and was listed in the Domesday Book, its jurisdiction including Withgill, Chaigley, Bashall, Waddington, West Bradford, Grindleton and, of course, Great Mitton itself. Although no trace has been found of the Saxon church, probably because it was constructed of wood, a Norman church certainly existed by 1103 with Ralph the Red as its Rector. This meant he could be Lord of the Manor, but he required an ordained priest to take the services. In 1215 the Rector chose to marry and this led to the church coming under control of the monks of Cockersand near Lancaster. What the monks of Whalley thought about this is not recorded.

All Hallows was begun around 1270, the chancel being added about twenty-five years later. Very little has been done to the body of the church since, proving how well it must have been built in the first place. The tower dates to 1438, there are Jacobean pews dating to the early 1600s, and the chancel screen made of wood and cast iron is thought to have been brought to Mitton from Sawley Abbey following its dissolution around 1536. The real joy of the church, however, is the Shireburn Chapel. The Shireburns of Stonyhurst added the chapel around 1440 and could claim a direct descent from the first Rector, Ralph the Red of Mytton. Ralph had a son called Jordan whose two sons Otto and Hugh divided the estate on the death of their father. Otto took Bailey and Aighton and Hugh took the Mitton area. At this time Otto changed his name to Otto de Bailey. By 1377 a descendant had changed the spelling of his name to Richard Bayley, and there is still a hostelry in Hurst Green called the Bayley Arms. He married Margaret Shireburn, and their son Richard for some reason preferred to change his name to that of his mother. Here, then, is the origin of the Shireburn family commemorated by the effigies in their chapel. Sir Richard Shireburn and his wife Maude are portrayed in a fine alabaster memorial, an example of the exquisite work of the sculptor Roilly of Burton. On the north wall of the chapel are the memorials to four generations of Richard Shireburns which were the work of William Stanton in the year 1699 at a cost of £253.

Downstream from Mitton is Ribchester, which proves that it is possible to achieve a perfect blend of ancient history and tourism. The riverside walks are spectacularly beautiful, there are plenty of car parks, three good inns and a number of restaurants. The area is flat and therefore ideal for the disabled.

The parish church of St Wilfrid may well have existed before the thirteenth century but there is no direct evidence. The discovery of some pre-Conquest crosses would suggest, but does not prove, that there was a Saxon church on the site. St Wilfrid was first the Bishop of Ripon and then the Archbishop of York who in A D 664 took a prominent role in the Synod of Whitby. This was a meeting of Celtic missionaries, who were often fierce warriors, and the more saint-like missionaries from Rome. The Roman view prevailed and set the pattern for church administration for the next thousand years.

Long before this, however, the Romans had a fort at Ribchester which they called Bremetannacum. A visit to the museum will transport you back to Roman Britain. During the 1990s the museum is undergoing a rebuilding and expanding programme, but the honorary curator Jim Ridge told us that funding is always a problem. Those of us who live north of the Wash wonder whether the museum would be short of

Two views of Preston in the 1830s. *Above* shows the country-town atmosphere of the market place before Gilbert Scott's 1867 town hall replaced the Georgian structure. We actually prefer the original. The print *below* shows Preston across the navigable river, with both chimney stacks and windmills a feature.

funds if it were situated in the south-east of England. This invaluable museum is one of the finest interpreters of the history of Roman Britain. It is a shame that an ornate helmet, the finest discovery around the site, is now in the British Museum with Ribchester having to make do with a replica.

A more modern gem is the Museum of Childhood, and entering this is like going back to the days of the Victorian music hall – all red velvet, stirring music and bright lights. It is housed in the old Co-op building and it is difficult to take in everything on one visit. There is a working model of Churchers' fairground, the original Professor Tomlin's world-famous Flea Circus, with an accompanying video showing the professor himself working at Belle Vue, Manchester in the 1960s, now with a commetary by Sid James.

There is a shop and a cafe in the museum, but anyone needing something stronger should visit The White Bull Hotel, the porch of which is supported by a couple of impressively solid Roman pillars. On the outskirts of Ribchester is Stydd, which has alms houses and a chapel which was erected by the Knights Hospitallers in early Norman times.

As the Ribble winds its way towards Preston there is another building which has something different to offer.

Do you like old houses? If yes, come to Samlesbury! Do you like antique shops? If yes, come to Samlesbury! Do you like your old houses to be neat and tidy? If yes, then stay away from Samlesbury! The fourteenth-century Hall is situated just on the busy A59 between Preston and Blackburn and just off Junction 31 of the M6 motorway.

Samlesbury Hall is an example of what can be done to protect our heritage by dedicated folk, without any financial assistance apart from our entrance fees and the subscriptions of the Friends of Samlesbury Hall. The best way to understand how close this place came to being lost is to trace its history.

When Robert the Bruce and his Scots burned down the old wood hall of Samlesbury around 1320, the Southworth family considered that their position close to the crossing of the River Ribble was far too dangerous. They built their new hall well away in what was then a large woodland which provided protection. Although now overlooked by the British Aircraft Corporation works and the A59, the Hall was then out in the wilds. The Southworths were then some distance from the attractive parish church of St Leonard the Less. The New Hall built in the old days would have consisted of a hall and a central fire with the smoke escaping (mostly) through a hole in the ceiling.

By 1550 the Southworth family had benefited from many years of Tudor-inspired peace and their dwelling surrounded by a moat reflected their affluence. The drawbridge was more for effect than for defence. The chapel was added in 1420 and had an entrance from the north side. This has now been closed as the chapel was eventually joined to the main house. There is a balcony which was used by the family whilst the estate workers used the floor of the chapel. The Southworths were ardent Catholics, and this accounts for the presence of a stone-mullioned Gothic window brought from Whalley Abbey following its dissolution in 1537 and also for the presence of a priest hole above the oriel window. It was their stout – many would say fearless – defence of the Catholic faith which led to their demise. Sir John Southworth was imprisoned in Manchester betwen 1581 and 1584, and when the tired old man died in 1595, the fortunes of the family were already on the slide. By 1678, with their faith intact but their fortunes in tatters, the Southworths sold out to Thomas Braddyll.

The Braddylls never used Samlesbury as a home but simply stripped most of its assets and removed them to their home at Conishead near Ulverston. Samlesbury was then let out as tenements to weavers and even had a period as an inn when the turnpike road was opened early in the nineteenth century. The building was in a shocking state of repair at this time, the moat having been drained, leaving a morass of puddles. At this stage it would not have been surprising if the Hall had declined gradually towards demolition, but it was saved first by one tragic man and then by an enlightened group. From the 1870s Joseph Harrison restored the Hall and entertained many famous guests including Charles Dickens. Joseph, however, overstretched himself and, in financial ruin, committed suicide. The Hall was under threat once more until the Samlesbury Hall Trust was set up, and they still manage it.

The first impression you get on entering is one of chaos – but organised chaos! Thanks to the Braddylls, there is no old furniture here except the antiques which are on sale. People bring their pieces to this permanent 'antiques roadshow', have them valued and may then put them up for sale. The Hall takes a percentage and thus adds to the much-needed revenue.

There is an air of dedicated realism from the administrators here. They point out that a popular feature of the Great Hall known as the Minstrels' Gallery is probably not what it appears. The gallery was fashioned from an ancient passage screen which once stood in the Hall. It does not seem that it was ever actually used as a minstrels' gallery but it certainly looks delightful. There are, however, areas of the building which are original including the fireplace, above which are the carved coats of arms of the Southworths and the Harrisons. In our view the destruction caused by the Braddylls has been gradually repaired by the work of the Hall Trust. The antique salerooms breathe life, the excellent tea room specialises in home-made produce, and there is a friendly atmosphere underlined by a notice on the grand piano inviting people to play it.

From the outside you can see how well the entrance fees have been spent, and the place looks as well as it has done for centuries. Occasionally visitors can enjoy watching the Bowmen of Pendle practise their skills on the archery field which has been in use since the days of Agincourt.

Between Samlesbury and Preston on the banks of the Ribble in the 1820s a couple of farm labourers dug up the Cuerdale Hoard. This was a chest full of Viking coins, ingots and silver ornaments, none dated later than AD 903. Why it was buried here we shall never know, but as we northerners might expect, most of the treasure is now in London's British Museum with the Harris Museum in Preston being allowed to keep a small selection. There may have been a settlement at Walton-Le-Dale which certainly had a substantial Roman settlement close to the junction of the Darwen with the Ribble.

This leaves Preston, now the administrative centre for much of Lancashire, and it is fitting that this book ends here having started in Manchester. Preston, or Priest-town, has medieval origins although most traces of these have been swamped beneath buildings typical of a cotton town. There are no stately homes within its boundaries although Hoghton Tower and

Samlesbury Hall were both within range of Preston. The street names, however, are a reminder of its past with Fishergate, Friargate and Stoneygate still the main thoroughfares, although the gentry of the seventeenth century would hardly recognise it.

It was at Preston in 1648 that Cromwell's forces inflicted a final and devastating defeat on the Royalists, and the town also played host to Bonnie Prince Charlie in 1745. This was a catholic town which was overtaken from the end of the eighteenth century by the Industrial Revolution. Richard Arkwright was born in Preston in 1732 and invented the spinning frame in 1769 which literally revolutionised the industry, thus laying the foundation for Preston's first cotton mill built by John Horrocks, from which he built up his own Cottonopolis.

What became the Horrocks-Crewdson Mills began with Horrocks cornering the handloom cottagers and bringing them under one roof. Other Lancashire businessmen did the same thing, but what John Horrocks did differently was to combine the spinning and weaving operations on the same campus, enabling him to take in raw cotton and deliver the finished article. This is why the firm became the largest of its kind in the world and why Preston became so prosperous.

The heart of the town is still the Market Square which we feel is one of the most impressive in England. It is overlooked by the Harris Museum and Art Gallery which opened in 1893 and was funded by Edmund R. Harris, a local man made good. It is very reminiscent of the British Museum in London, its fluted columns giving the square the feel of a Roman forum. The building contains a collection of nineteenth and twentieth-century paintings as well as ceramics, glass and costume. There is also a well-displayed collection of the work of poet Francis Thompson (1859-1905), a Roman Catholic doctor, and a drug addict, who was born at No 7 Winckley Street. The Harris Museum has its own shop and cafe.

Until the early 1980s Preston had important docks, but these are not used for industrial purposes any more, with the result that the river flowing to the coast is gradually and perhaps permanently silting them up. Stranded in the docks is the old Isle of Man ferryboat, *The Manxman*, now used as a nightclub.

A riverside marina is developing, however, which is ideal for watersports including windsurfing and sailing.

Preston has two other attractions of a more leisurely nature. Those who enjoy stargazing should visit the Moor Park Observatory managed by the School of Physics and Astronomy of Lancashire Polytechnic. It is open on at least two Fridays per month between September and March except for December – with visiting times being between 7.30pm and 9.30pm. Also there is the Regimental Museum of the North Lancashire Regiment which is situated at Fulwood Barracks and open all year on Tuesdays and Thursdays.

The Guild Hall and Charter Theatre were built to celebrate Preston's 1972 Guild. Preston Guild, a magnificent occasion, gives the town an excuse to spend money and recoup some of it in the course of the jamboree which it generates. The event takes place every twenty years and gives rise to the Lancashire saying, when you lend something of value, 'I suppose I'll get it back next Preston Guild'. The institution originally had a very serious purpose, and many prominent towns had their guilds aimed at fostering honesty, fair dealing and top-quality workmanship. Although there may have been an even earlier origin, probably as early as 1179, a guild was certainly held at Preston on June 27th 1328. It prevented cheats from presenting second-rate services, the Guild being a union of men sworn to fair dealing. They operated from what amounted to their own weights and measures office, known as their Guild Hall. They were also insurance companies because any member taken ill and unable to work was looked after. On the other hand the members also had responsibilities: each member had to serve a seven-year apprenticeship, and substandard workmanship or cheating was punishable by expulsion.

The coming of the Industrial Revolution when 'Britain's bread hangs by Preston's thread' brought the demise of the Guilds, but thankfully the ceremony was retained as a link with the past.

Although medieval Preston has gone, there are still some Georgian houses in the Avenham area overlooking the park on the banks of the Ribble.

Proud Preston is therefore an ideal place to complete this

book, although, given Lancashire's rich and diverse heritage, we are aware as much of what we have had to leave out as we are of what has been included. Still, we would not like to know everything, for this way we have much more travelling and exploring in our native county to look forward to.

Further Reading

Armstrong, Thomas (1947) *King Cotton* (Collins)
Biddle, Gordon (1980) *Lancashire Waterways* (Dalesman)
Freethy, Ron *The River Mersey* (Terence Dalton)
Freethy, Ron *The River Ribble* (Terence Dalton)
Gillies A.D. (1988) *Wigan, Through Wickham's Window* (Phillimore)
Greenwood, Walter (1951) *Lancashire* (Robert Hale)
Kennedy, Michael (1970) *Portrait of Manchester* (Robert Hale)
Lofthouse, Jessica (1974) *Lancashire Countrygoer* (Robert Hale)
Longmate, Norman (1978) *The Hungry Mills, The Story of the Lancashire Cotton Famine 1861-5* (Temple Smith)
McNight, Hugh (1978) *The Shell Book of Inland Waterways* (David and Charles)
Makepeace, Chris (1983) *The Manchester Ship Canal* (Hendon)
Millward, Roy (1955) *Lancashire: An Illustrated lecture on the history of the Landscape* (Hodder and Stoughton)
Waugh, Edwin (1870) *Besom Ben Stories* (John Heywood)
Waugh, Edwin (1871) *Lancashire Sketches* (John Heywood)

Index